Classic Accidents

David Farmer BA LLB FInstPet MIOSH

Croner Publications Ltd
Croner House
London Road
Kingston upon Thames
Surrey KT2 6SR
Tel: 01-547 3333

Copyright © 1989 Kingwood
This edition first published 1989
Reprinted 1990

Published by
Croner Publications Ltd,
Croner House,
London Road,
Kingston upon Thames
Surrey KT2 6SR
Telephone: 01-547 3333

While every care has been taken
in the writing and editing of this book,
readers should be aware that only Acts of Parliament
and Statutory Instruments have the force of law,
and that only the courts can authoritatively
interpret the law.

British Library Cataloguing in Publication Data

Farmer, David, *1928* –
Classic accidents – (Croner health and
safety guides)
1. Great Britain. Factories. Accidents.
Causes & prevention
I. Title
363.1'17'0941

ISBN 1-85452-011-3

Contents

Introduction

This book is not about the law of occupational health and safety. Nor is it about the legal (either civil or criminal) consequences of the incidents related in its pages. It is not a comprehensive guide to all the practical precautions which, if followed, would prevent the accidents it describes.

It is an attempt to make the reader aware of some particular sorts of occupational hazards without having to have personal and direct experience of them before taking the steps necessary to prevent them at the place of work.

The accidents are described as "classic" because they are being repeated over and over again. They have become an established part of the workplace accident scene. This is as depressing as it is unnecessary and avoidable.

Details surrounding the central accident cause vary enormously but the core theme remains tragically constant. Consider the seven classics:

(a) people getting caught up in machinery with rotating parts by their hair or things they wear;
(b) people falling while using ladders;
(c) reversing vehicles colliding with those unseen in their path;
(d) people being burnt due to ignorance of the hazardous characteristics of flammable liquids they handle or use;
(e) people being overcome in confined spaces through gassing and asphyxiation and the deaths of those who try to rescue them;
(f) slipping, tripping and falling accidents;
(g) accidents occurring during maintenance operations.

The choice of these seven classic accident types has been prompted not only by frequency of occurrence (their inclusion would be justified by this alone), but also because each class illustrates a particular aspect of a system of work. The main challenge to every level of management is the establishment and maintenance of a safe system of work. The accidents written about all reflect the significance of a particular facet of this challenge.

The author is indebted to various official publications for extracts from which he has taken most of the case histories. These include the Health and Safety Executive's *Agriculture – Health and Safety 1982–83*; the Factory Inspectorate's former magazine *Accidents* (of which the author was editor); HSE reports *Transport Kills; Deadly Maintenance; Dangerous Maintenance – A study of maintenance accidents in the chemical industry and how to prevent them; Watch your step — Prevention of slipping, tripping and falling accidents at work* and data provided by the Factory Inspectorate's Accident Prevention Advisory Unit (APAU).

Many of the incidents described in the book had fatal consequences. It has to be remembered, however, that for everyone killed in a particular type of workplace accident there are many others who are seriously hurt by the same types of incidents and an even greater number who suffer minor injuries.

No attempt has been made to make the few measurements in the text uniformly metric or imperial. In no instance was the measurement a crucial issue but it is given purely as an indication of scale.

The chapter on accidents in the office is a departure from the normal pattern. Office accidents are characterised mainly by their diversity and not, for the most part, their severity, so the intention has been to present a wider variety of case histories to illustrate this. Even so, readers will see that two of the office accident case histories fall into the classic category covered in Chapters 2 and 6. There are examples of hair entanglement in unguarded machinery, and fumes in a confined space causing a death from asphyxiation. What was not normally thought of as a confined space had become one when a boiler flue became blocked.

Although office accidents have many varied causes, falls and handling mishaps feature as prominently there as in other workplaces. Here the guidance in the chapter on slips, trips and falls is relevant as much in offices as anywhere else. The book concludes with a brief chapter on accident prevention management where a number of basic points, to be included in a prevention strategy, are emphasised.

Chapter 11 is by way of being a postscript. It looks at potential accident victims and what special characteristics may need to be taken into account. For example: the young are vulnerable through inexperience, while the old are prone to accident through failing to act quickly enough. Managers are gently reminded that precautions are just as much for them as for those they manage.

Chapter 1

Classic accidents defined

Those who actually witness accidents are forewarned and made aware of the hazards responsible for them. By utilising our collective experience of particular types of commonly recurring accidents we can publicise the common causes. This will enable appropriate remedial action to be planned and further repetition of the "classic" accidents can be avoided.

Introduction

Why is the word "classic" used in the title of the book? Among its several meanings is "a model of its kind" and also "something of lasting interest or significance". Both of these definitions are relevant to the choice of title.

All of the accidents described in the book are hardy perennials — they are models of their kind. They keep on happening to different people, at different times and in different places. Unfortunately there does not yet appear to be, judging from the available evidence, a general ability or willingness to learn from the past experiences of others in matters of accident causation and prevention. It is in an attempt to change this that this book has been written by presenting the collective experience of certain common mishaps. Once there is awareness of a hazard the means of eliminating or controlling it are relatively simple. Without awareness the toll of accidents will continue at great personal and economic cost to all those concerned, employees and employers alike.

Individual experience

As individuals, if we have seen with our own eyes someone's scalp wrapped tightly round a drill spindle and have witnessed the victim's distress, pain and permanent disfigurement, we appreciate the gravity of the hazard of entanglement and do something about it.

Again, if we know of a relative or friend who died trying in vain to rescue an unconscious colleague from a fume-filled tank, we attempt in our own sphere of control or influence, to take steps to ensure that such an event could never happen to us or to those who are in our charge. It appears, however, that unless we have such direct personal experiences (or ones affecting someone very close to us such as a relative, neighbour or acquaintance) there is a strong possibility that we will remain indifferent to the hazards through ignorance of them and hence of the precautions which could so easily be taken to avoid them.

Why the choice of these particular classic accidents? Firstly, they are all common in workplaces across the world. Secondly, they underline the importance of certain general principles of accident prevention which every management should espouse. The principles certainly have much wider applications than just to the accidents described here to illustrate them.

Accident prevention principles

Each accident category has a lesson beyond that implicit in its particular facts.

The chapter on machinery entanglement accidents emphasises that individuals need to be aware of specific types of machine danger (not just generalised ones) and to tailor (quite literally) their dress and personal adornments accordingly. Dressing for the job is an important part of working safely. The chapter on ladder mishaps invites everyone to think closely about alternative and safer work methods rather than adopt unthinkingly the ubiquitous, cheap, readily available but much more risky first option. The chapter covering the reversing vehicle menace serves to underline the possibility of doing away with a hazard by eliminating the need for the activity which creates it. Failing this, the chapter looks at resorting to modern technology to devise aids to accident avoidance and to the role of effective training and supervision of the human participants in the averting of dangers. The chapter on flammable liquids clearly emphasises how important it is to know in some detail about the physical characteristics of what is stored, conveyed and used in the workplace. All the accidents described are directly attributable to a human failure to appreciate the significance of these characteristics. Chapter 6 deals with areas of ignorance about less obvious and insidious hazards associated with confined spaces. In addition to considering the dangers themselves the importance of having a well thought out and rehearsed work plan, including a contingency element to cope if things go wrong, is emphasised.

Chapter 7 is about slips, trips and falls, to which the elderly are particularly, but not exclusively, prone and concerns mundane but often overlooked subjects such as cleaning, keeping clear and repairing floors. This category of mishap accounts for a worrying one in five of all accidents reported to the authorities.

Chapters 8 and 9 concern accidents during maintenance operations and accidents in the office environment respectively. Many of these are variants of the classic types. Chapter 10 is a summary of accident prevention management.

The final chapter is a postscript. It is a reminder that it is people who fall victim to accidents, and points out that there are certain classes of people who need to be catered for in a special way. This is so because they are young, brash, energetic and unthinking; or, old, frail, hard of hearing or just cussed; or, handicapped, either mentally or physically and hence needing special attention in certain areas; or, last but not least, in senior positions and perhaps harbouring false ideas about their invincibility, or foolishly believing that nothing can possibly happen to them because of who they are.

Safe systems of work

The book has deliberately made no references to any specific legal requirements, but implicit in all the tragedies it unfolds is the central core of every legal control regime — the duty of every management to establish and maintain safe systems of work.

This implies comprehensive hazard identification at the workplace and the allocation of sufficient resources to contain the hazards identified. This in turn covers adequate attention to machinery, plant and equipment; to substances stored, conveyed and used; to good staff selection, training and supervision; to an effective system of monitoring and auditing the performance of everyone concerned, to see that the set standards and objectives are achieved.

The creation of awareness — the prime aim

The pattern followed in the book is to make brief introductory comments and then to present a few case histories illustrating the types of accident associated with each of the seven classic causes.

After the case histories there is a short section analysing the main factors involved in them, followed by some concluding commentary on precautionary measures.

No attempt has been made to dwell in detail on the precautionary measures because *the main purpose of the book is to create and foster awareness of classic causes of accidents which continue to happen too frequently.*

If machinery was always one hundred per cent guarded; ladders outlawed; vehicle reversing unnecessary; flammable liquids dealt with paying due regard to the behaviour of their vapours; confined spaces only entered by trained and properly equipped staff with colleagues on standby to cope quickly and efficiently with any emergencies — this book would not be necessary. It is necessary because the accidents described are still happening regularly in every type of work environment. They happen because there is no collective experience on which management can draw to indicate the relatively simple steps which can be taken to prevent the accidents written about in this book.

Management action plans

Each chapter ends with a brief management action plan which gives the main steps which can be taken to avoid these particular classic accidents.

Chapter 2

Machinery entanglement accidents

Direct contact with machine parts which cut, crush or abrade is quite readily understood. Not so the more insidious nature of entanglement which can start with just a wisp of hair or a few threads of cloth and end with the whole body of the victim being tightly caught up. Escape from entanglement is unusual and multiple, severe and often fatal injuries follow.

Introduction

Wherever there are moving parts of plant or machinery there is danger. Sometimes the danger is direct and immediate as where a sawyer slips when presenting a piece of wood to a circular saw blade and fingers come into contact with the fast-moving teeth of the saw. Anyone pointing out such dangers to a newcomer does not have to dwell long on the gory possibilities. They are nearly always self-evident and quickly understood.

What is not so obvious is the insidious nature of entanglement where the contact with the moving machinery is indirect, at least initially. The following typical case histories illustrate some of the ways that entanglement can occur.

Case histories

(a) *Turner entangled by spiral of swarf*

A turner working at an old, but still serviceable, centre-lathe was taking a light cut from a mild-steel bar to clean up its pitted surface. The spirals of swarf were coming off in long, quite springy coils. One of the coils made its way like a gimlet into the loose weave of the sleeve of the operator's woollen pullover. It held on for just long enough for the rest of the clothing to lap round and begin to tighten with the continued rotation of the bar in the lathe chuck. The lathe was fitted with a knock-off bar which the operator's body bumped against. Although the lathe stopped quite quickly the entanglement had involved the garment, skin and tissues, and the operator's arm was very severely injured.

(b) *Pillar drill scalped youth*

A pillar drill with its $2_{1/4}$ inch diameter spindle rotating at about 200 rpm, was not fitted with any guard over a length of about 9 inches. The exposed, vertical spindle was at a height of about 5 feet above the floor. The machine was fitted with a $_{1/4}$ inch diameter drill bit, which was being used to make a series of holes in chipboard. The operator, a boy of 16, was leaning forward to watch the progress of the job. A wisp of his, at that time, fashionably long hair lapped round the rotating spindle just above the drill chuck. Despite an instant response to the sensation of tugging, the boy lost a significant portion of his

14

scalp from the crown of his head as he pulled himself free. He now has to wear a wig.

(c) *Glove entwined before drill trip device operated*

While drilling the third of a number of holes in the top flanges of some joists, the operator swept a hand across the surface to clear away an accumulation of swarf. The operator wore gloves for protection against dirt and cuts. They had leather palms and cotton backs and cuffs. The cuffs were caught up by the drill, rotating at 200 rpm. They acted as a ligature which, with entrapped swarf, caused injuries which later necessitated surgery to remove a damaged finger. The only thing which prevented much more serious injuries was the operation of a trip device which stopped the drill. This would have worked more quickly had it been adjusted properly. It would also have worked more quickly but for the fact that entanglement continued through 180° rather than the normal 90° which would have been the case had the operator not had to change from the normal operating position because of the length of the joists being drilled.

(d) *Ring caught by drill amputated finger*

While deburring small holes in mild steel components a woman was using a fairly high speed bench mounted drilling machine. As she swept a hand across the drill table to move aside accumulated workpieces the drill point caught in her wedding ring. The injuries sustained to the flesh and tendons of her finger were such that surgical amputation was necessary at hospital.

(e) *Abrasive disc wound up in tie*

A portable electric drilling machine fitted with a flexible abrasive disc instead of a drill bit was being used to clean up the surface of a weld joining two sheet metal parts together. As the operator leaned over the job his dangling tie became caught up round the short length of spindle between the drill chuck and the rubber-backed abrasive pad. The machinery literally wound itself up the tie, but before the abrasive disc came to a stop it inflicted severe facial injuries on the operator.

Analysis

Wherever there are rotating parts of power driven machinery on static or mobile plant; whether they rotate quickly or slowly; whether they are smooth, threaded, or have projections such as keys or set-screws; or whether the exposed lengths are long or short, such parts are dangerous. Examples of typical rotating parts, irrespective of the plane in which they rotate, are stockbars, spindles, chucks, couplings, mandrels and shafts.

Rotation needs to continue for only a few seconds for the most severe of injuries to occur. Even when the power has been switched off, either by the operation of the normal machine controls or by emergency trip devices, injuries may be inflicted before the parts lose their momentum and come to rest.

In the case histories, the agents initiating entanglement were the sleeve of a woollen garment, long hair, a glove, a wedding ring and a tie. These are examples only. Other adornments and items of clothing can equally easily precipitate the initial entanglement: loose or frayed cuffs; torn flaps of material, pockets or belts; bandages; scarves; hair ribbons; jewellery; loose coats, aprons, skirts and so on.

The awareness of danger which has to be firmly established and sustained is that anything loose upon a person can become entangled with rotating machine parts and lead to injury. It is not always necessary for there to be direct and conscious initial contact. Machinery in motion may create air movement which attracts the first contact with hair or loose fabric. The first lap round is the crucial one. Once that which has been caught is held, the wrapping caused by the machine's continued rotation is virtually unstoppable. Clothes, limbs and entire bodies can be involved in the entanglement and very severe injuries sustained. A fatal outcome is not infrequent.

Precautionary measures

(a) *Statutory controls*

Most countries include as part of their statutory control regimes in the workplace, some edict calling for the guarding of dangerous machinery. The test applied by the courts in the United Kingdom to establish danger is a useful one to use here.

Machinery is defined as dangerous if it might be a "reasonably foreseeable cause of injury to anybody acting in a way in which a human being may be reasonably expected to act in circumstances which may be reasonably expected to occur".

Whilst normal approach is the main criterion, it must never be overlooked that people very often act in a way which is unreasonable. This means that those trying to anticipate how people and machinery come into close and often tragic proximity should not confine themselves to considering what they think is reasonable and in line with the instructions and training of those concerned.

As was said by a judge in one significant judgement in a machinery accident case when considering people's behaviour, "such behaviour as is reasonably foreseeable is not necessarily confined to such behaviour as is reasonable behaviour". Just because someone does something stupid whereby he or she suffers injury, it must not be assumed that the machinery responsible for causing the injury is not dangerous under normal circumstances.

(b) *Practical safeguards*

In the prevention of entanglement the principle of guarding is simple — complete enclosure. Of course the application of the principle can pose problems. One such is the example of a rotating threaded shaft along which some other part moves. Sleeves of concertina-like construction over the shaft can overcome this at the slight cost of losing a small amount of traverse at the point where the sleeve is secured at each end of the shaft. Another whole group of examples is where machine tools, such as drilling machines and lathes, have rotating parts the working ends of which (drills or workpieces) have necessarily to be exposed to enable the work to be accomplished.

Failing complete enclosure, in some instances distance guarding will keep machine and operator, or passer-by, sufficiently far apart to prevent either contact or entry into the zone where machine movement creates enough air turbulence to attract such items as long hair or loose clothing.

Another occasionally acceptable alternative is the use of a quick-acting, properly adjusted trip device which stops machine movement in the earliest stages of entanglement before serious injury occurs. However, it has been seen, in the case histories given, that such devices are limited in their ability to prevent injury.

(c) *Correct dress*

Dressing appropriately for whatever job is being done is an important part of the work system. A footballer, surgeon, and circus clown can all be instantly recognised by their dress. In each case dress performs a vital function in the job the wearer is undertaking. It should be no different for those who work with machinery.

It is clear that there has to be an appreciation by those concerned that the wearing of scarves, gloves, or jewellery (even wedding rings) is unacceptably dangerous. It is also implied that workrooms need to be warm enough to make scarves unnecessary, and that methods for swarf removal other than the use of a gloved hand should be available. How to part someone from a wedding ring is yet a further problem. A good standard of close-fitting garment, devoid of parts which hang loose, is essential. Good care of the garment throughout its life, with facilities for repair, button replacement and eventual renewal by a simple procedure is counselled. Short hair can be encouraged, but long hair *must* be tucked away. If the reason for the imposition is made clear user resistance can usually be overcome.

Management action plan

(a) Identify all rotating parts of machinery capable of causing entanglement.

(b) Consider all possible reasons anyone may have to approach machines, not forgetting visiting contractors' employees. Do not overlook careless, negligent, or even unreasonable approaches.

(c) Adopt the most appropriate and effective system of physical guarding for the machinery parts concerned.

(d) Make sure everyone at risk knows the exact nature of the dangers of entanglement and the items which can easily precipitate it.

(e) Ensure all staff who may be exposed to dangers of entanglement are dressed suitably. Establish procedures for the checking, renewal and care of all workwear involved.

Chapter 3

Accidents with ladders

Ladders, though versatile and convenient, are not renowned for a good safety record. If they must be used there are several fundamental rules which should always be applied and a number of ancillary items of equipment which can reduce the risks associated with ladders used either as means of access, or as a place of work.

Introduction

It is not really surprising that the ladder is such a universally popular tool. It is convenient, versatile, light and portable, and relatively cheap. It is not only used as a means of access to workplaces, it is also used as a workplace in its own right. It is, however, a tool with another rather sombre characteristic: it is involved in a great number of accidents.

In this chapter this unpalatable aspect is examined more closely.

Case histories

(a) *Fatal fall when ladder slipped*

A joiner fell 4.5m to his death into a concrete tank. He was climbing into the tank using an untied ladder. The foot of the ladder slipped. He was working for a company constructing a new pumping station forming part of a drainage scheme. The floor of the tank was dished and coated with a gloss paint. The ladder had been positioned by the deceased who was an experienced worker, but he had neither been authorised nor instructed to go into the tank. The reason for him climbing into the tank remained a mystery.

(b) *Overreached from untied ladder*

A contracts manager with a painting company fell over 7 m from an untied extension ladder. The ladder was nearly 9 m long. The man overreached himself and the untied ladder moved slightly. He had been recently appointed contracts manager and spent some time painting but most of the time supervising contracts. He made his own arrangements about how the work should be done. He had elected to use the ladder for the job he was doing when he fell and died of the injuries sustained.

(c) *Ladder and scaffold tower fell*

A partner in a painting firm was working from a tower scaffold which fell over. He was fatally injured in a fall of about 6 m on to a concrete floor. He was working from a 3.6 m ladder supported on a scaffold tower, itself 3.6 m high. As he was trying to free a fanlight window the tower scaffold fell away from the building. Neither tower scaffold nor ladder were tied.

(d) *Electric drill shock caused fall from ladder*

While drilling a hole in a wall into which a bracket fixing was to be plugged, a carpenter experienced an electric shock from the drill he was using . The shock caused him to drop the drilling machine and also to fall a distance of 4 m from the ladder on which he was standing. He fell into fairly soft soil and was only badly bruised. He had been using both hands to hold the drill and exert the necessary pressure.

(e) *Ladder rungs rotten*

A wooden ladder, retrieved from a client's factory yard, was pressed into service by visiting television aerial installers because their own metal extension ladder was not quite long enough to reach one spot where they wanted to secure part of the cable-run to the aerial.

The ladder was heavy but they managed to put it into place and, while one man footed the ladder to stop it from slipping, his colleague climbed up it and secured it by tying it to a metal downpipe with a short length of aerial cable.

Satisfied that safe access was assured, one of the aerial fitters obtained a coil of cable, which he put over his shoulder in order to leave both hands free for the climb. All the hand tools he was likely to need were snug in their purpose-made holder attached to his belt. When he was halfway up the ladder, one of the rungs gave way without warning and the fitter fell to the ground, breaking a leg and sustaining severe bruising to his body.

Later examination of what had appeared to be a sound and safe ladder revealed four or five suspect rungs in the vicinity of the one that broke; all these rungs showed signs of rot. The ladder had not been used by the factory staff for as long as anyone could remember.

(f) *Ladder trampolines*

Painters who were painting two adjacent tanks at a dyeworks decided to get from one tank to the other by laying a ladder between the two and placing a plank along its rungs. The distance between the tanks was a little longer than the longest plank or staging they had with them on the site.

The makeshift access was effectively only the width of the plank, but the painters were used to such walkways and used it for two or three days without incident. On one occasion, a painter carrying a pot of paint in each hand, moved across quite briskly which caused the ladder to move up and down like a trampoline. The painter, thinking he was about to be thrown off, deliberately jumped to the ground about ten feet below. He sprained both ankles quite badly when he landed. He had, surprisingly, not let go of the paint pots when he jumped and the paint from one splashed over his face and into his eyes, causing irritation and discomfort for several weeks.

Analysis

Whilst there are any number of variations on the common theme there are only four main precipitating causes for ladder accidents. The ladder may be defective and break. A United Kingdom survey in 1971 revealed that only about 5% of ladder accidents were caused in this way. The ladder may slip to left or right at its top point of rest and fall with its user after the point of balance has been passed. The ladder may slip out from the base and ladder and user fall together. The user of the ladder may do a job with both hands and something happens to upset his or her foothold, causing a fall from the ladder. The survey mentioned earlier found that just over 40% of ladder accidents fell into this last category.

It is highly unlikely that the ladder will ever be totally outlawed. It is equally unlikely that the use of ladders will ever be totally safe. Just consider dispassionately some of its fundamental inadequacies. As a means of access the ladder foothold is not ideal. It is a small area of rung on to which is placed a much larger area of foot. Either the rungs or the user's shoes (or both) may be wet, muddy, slippery, or sticky. The handholds are the sides of the ladder which are almost invariably larger in cross-section than can be grasped easily with optimum comfort and an efficient firm grip. During climbing, only one hand and one foot are in contact with the ladder at the same time. If either slips the chance of an accident happening is much increased.

As a workplace the rung is a small and uncomfortable resting place for the insteps carrying the whole body's weight, plus anything that is being carried by the user. This is especially the case where the job takes any length of time. By definition too if a ladder is a workplace it means that both hands are frequently engaged in doing the job concerned and are not available for holding on. These are not good portents for safe use, even when the ladder itself is in excellent condition and securely tied in position or otherwise firmly secured against any kind of slipping.

Precautionary measures

(a) *Use alternatives*
It has to be said that the only effective way of eliminating ladder accidents is to eliminate ladders. The first step in any campaign to avoid ladder accidents, therefore, is to see if there is another feasible way of gaining access, or another suitable workplace to use for the task envisaged.

Lift truck platforms, mast work platforms, scaffold towers suitably stable and secured are some examples of alternatives offering better stability and safety. This assumes, of course, that permanent stairways with wide treads and handrails are not a possible and preferable alternative. There are many examples of ladders being replaced by permanent, protected stairways (eg: providing access to overhead crane cabs).

(b) *Good standards*
If a ladder is the only feasible tool to be used in any particular case, then it should be of a good standard (either wood or metal) and maintained in good repair. To this end a regular, routine, simply documented system of examination and inspection should be implemented.

(c) *Secure fixing*
No ladder should be used unless it is securely tied so that it can not slip to either side at its top point of rest. Where the ladder's top point of rest proves to be unsuitable (because it is brittle or fragile or lacks rigidity) it is possible to use a ladder stay. This holds the ladder out at a distance from the unsuitable resting point and utilises the rigid vertical surface as a resting point instead. Similarly, all ladders should be secured against slipping out from the base. To this latter end there should be strict compliance with the 1 in 4 rule. Abiding by this rule achieves for the ladder its safest angle of repose, which is about 75° to the horizontal (ie about 1 m out for every 4 m in height).

Two problems have to be solved as far as ladder tying is concerned. The first is to be sure there is something suitable to tie the ladder to. Whatever is used as an anchor point to tie a ladder to must itself be secure and, in the absence of a suitably strong and rigid point of attachment already in existence where the ladder rests, one should be provided by the person using the ladder (eg a screw-eye into wood or brickwork through which a tie can be passed and secured).

The second is to ensure the ladder is stable when someone climbs it to secure the tie in the first place, or unties the lashing when the job is completed. At this vulnerable time a second person is needed to hold the ladder. This solution, however, is not feasible where the ladder is more than about 5 m long. Beyond this length of ladder it is not possible to hold it if it starts to slip with someone standing on it near the top.

(d) *Ancillary equipment*

Use should be made of the various ancillary items of equipment which afford a higher standard of safe working. Such items include "ladder jacks" (these are adjustable extension devices securely fixed to the ladder stiles which enable them to be at different levels so that ladders may safely be footed on slopes or staircases); non-slip feet (never to be entirely relied on as alternatives to the use of secure ties); clip-on platforms which attach to rungs providing a more generous area of working platform and comfort for the user's feet.

(e) *Miscellaneous*

A number of miscellaneous points need to be considered and users of ladders made aware of them so that the system of work of which they form a part is as safe as it can reasonably be made.

(i) Metal ladders need to be handled very carefully wherever there is the possibility of accidental contact with live, uncovered electrical conductors.

(ii) Where fixed metal ladders are the only appropriate means of access, safety hoops should be fitted if the ladders concerned are more than about 2 m high.

(iii) Ladders should never be supported on their rungs. Only the ladder stiles are designed and made to provide support. Equally, the rungs should not be used as supports for boards.

(iv) Fixed or portable ladders should always rise at least 1.05 m above the top place of landing.

(v) Sections of extension ladders should overlap by $1_{1/2}$ rungs in the case of a 5 m long ladder; $2_{1/2}$ rungs with a 5–6 m ladder; $3_{1/2}$ rungs with a ladder over 6 m long. (NB the ladder lengths given are their closed lengths.)

(vi) It should never be forgotten by ladder users that when they are standing on their ladders they may be closer to other hazards such as overhead transmission shafting; electrically live, uninsulated metalwork; or the travelling parts of overhead cranes than they would be if standing at ground level.

Management action plan

(a) Ensure all ladders are of a good standard initially; are properly stored when not in use; are subject to routine examination to see that they remain fit for use.

(b) Examine all tasks for which ladders are used and adopt alternative equipment and working methods where and when possible.

(c) When ladder use is unavoidable ensure that there are facilities for securing the ladder at top and bottom and that appropriate anchor points exist and are always used.

(d) Where the nature of the job and/or location prevents tying, instruct those concerned only to work with a second person holding the ladder.

(e) Use the ancillary aids which are available and a system for getting tools, equipment and materials up to the ladder user without endangering his or her hand or foot hold.

Chapter 4

Accidents with reversing vehicles

The visibility of drivers reversing their vehicles is notoriously poor and the manoeuvre has a high record of serious accidents. Reversing can sometimes be avoided but where this is not possible it can be suitably controlled by a variety of devices and/or the constant use of a properly trained banksman guiding the driver.

Introduction

The use of road transport vehicles within workplaces, involving both conventional and special purpose vehicles, has grown steadily over recent years. So has the number of accidents associated with them, many of which have fatal consequences for the victims.

One aspect in particular has created more than average concern because it is involved in between a fifth and a quarter of all the deaths attributable to transport mishaps according to a United Kingdom survey in 1978–80: this is the reversing of vehicles.

Two classes of vehicle are at the head of the list of those responsible: heavy goods lorries and lift trucks. But every type of vehicle is potentially more hazardous when moving backwards than when it is being driven in the direction where maximum visibility is normally provided. As will be seen later the avoidance of reversing accidents involves vehicle design, good planning of the traffic system and the training of both drivers and those others involved when vehicles travel in reverse.

Case histories

(a) *Reversing lorry crushed manager*

A long articulated lorry was reversing into a small factory yard with two people assisting the driver, one at the front and one, the manager, at the rear. The manager was crushed by the vehicle against a wall while holding open the yard door.

(b) *Shunting trailers killed yard worker*

Articulated lorries were shunting trailers about a works yard non-stop during the working day. So that the manoeuvre was done in a uniform and expert way one man did all the actual shunting himself. The trailers arrived loaded with empty barrels returned for refilling. Two yard workers unsheeted the loads of returned empties and sheeted over loads of full barrels ready for delivery. Late one summer's day one of the yard workers was found dead between two trailers. An empty barrel lay close by. Only one explanation was possible; the victim had been standing on the barrel to reach up to a tarpaulin to untie it when the trailers were shunted. The lorry had knocked him off but the driver had felt nothing. No one else saw or heard anything.

(c) *Refuse vehicle ran over outpatient*
A refuse collection vehicle was reversing in the grounds of a hospital when it ran over an outpatient and killed him. There was no banksman.

(d) *Reversing fork lift truck knocked over supervisor*
A forklift truck reversed into a corridor in a printing works through a canvas strip curtain, knocking over a supervisor. The truck had been travelling at walking pace and the driver sounded his horn but visibility through the curtain was poor.

(e) *Overturning mechanical shovel crushed driver*
The inadequately trained driver of a mechanical loading shovel reversed over the edge of an embankment of a motorway under construction. The machine overturned crushing the driver to death.

Analysis

Very few vehicles have good visibility for reversing manoeuvres. As a result, the practice has grown of using banksmen (ie: lookouts or guides) stationed in such positions that they can see where vehicles should be steered and give the drivers the appropriate directions. The aim is to move the vehicles without damaging them or property, or injuring any people in the process.

It has to be accepted that some reversing of vehicles is unavoidable and therefore careful consideration should be given to the precautions outlined below. Following them scrupulously could eliminate this cause of death and serious injury in the workplace.

Precautionary measures

(a) *Avoidance of reversing*
Wherever and whenever reversing of vehicles can be avoided it should be. As has already been seen it is a manoeuvre for which virtually no vehicle has been designed; it is much slower than the more familiar forward travel and it is far more dangerous.

29

How can reversing be avoided? Improving road layout to provide one way traffic systems and drive-through loading and unloading is often possible. In new facilities it can be specifically designed in at the drawing board.

If reversing can not be avoided, planning can still play a part in minimising the risk of mishaps. For example, the vehicular and pedestrian traffic can be effectively separated so that only those with direct and necessary duties in relation to the vehicles need to be near to them at all.

(b) *Vehicle design*

The principal drawback to safe reversing is the extremely poor visibility for drivers when vehicles move backwards. Apart from normal internal driving mirrors or those placed externally, a number of optical devices are available which enhance considerably the driver's field of vision. Fixed convex mirrors on buildings can also help, but sometimes the distortions at the edge of the circle can be difficult to interpret until the driver is used to them.

A problem with some vehicles when reversing into restricted areas is that they have to retract their mirrors to avoid them striking obstructions, thus losing even more visibility.

Some use of closed circuit television equipment is now being made to improve the driver's field of vision and this is likely to increase. Similarly the use of radar to detect obstructions has been tried with advantage.

Other devices rely not on vision but on touching obstructions, inanimate or human. They work on the principle of a hollow rubber tube "bumper" containing air at atmospheric pressure. If this is affected by impact a very sensitive air valve is actuated and applies the air brakes. The brakes are kept locked on until the truck is back in neutral. To move the vehicle at all a forward gear has to be selected. This device is especially useful where not only does the driver not see anything but is unlikely to feel anything as the vehicle "bumps" someone standing in the blind-spot area.

Yet one further device fitted to many vehicles is the audible warning device or klaxon which sounds its warning automatically when the vehicle is moving in reverse. Sometimes these are synchronised with flashing warning lights as well. There are, however, serious limitations.

Where more than one vehicle is concerned the noise can be misleading and confusing. Also, if the ambient noise level is high the sound of the warning klaxon may simply remain unheard or merge into the background din. Ironically if noise levels are high and ear defenders are worn they will cut out or attenuate all noise, including that giving warning of potential danger.

(c) *Banksmen*

The additions to the vehicle, however good, almost invariably need supplementing by a guide telling the driver what to do. In the United Kingdom survey mentioned earlier, three of the fatalities studied showed that it was the banksman himself who was the victim of the reversing vehicle which he should have been controlling safely.

Training of drivers and banksmen in the system adopted is essential. Where the latter stands; the unambiguous signals given to the driver; the stringently adhered-to principle that the driver stops the vehicle the instant the banksman disappears from the field of vision: these are all essential precautions to the successful and safe operation of the system of work.

Management action plan

(a) Make an appraisal of all traffic and the routes used and examine the possibilities of avoiding the reversing manoeuvre.

(b) Where vehicle reversing has to continue, ensure that vehicles are so equipped as to give the best driver-visibility achievable at the rear.

(c) Utilise mirrors on buildings and other suitable markings to assist drivers, especially those from other firms.

(d) Exclude non-participating pedestrians from reversing areas.

(e) Train and brief banksmen to guide drivers reversing and prohibit reversing without the use of their services.

(f) Rigidly enforce the rule that no vehicle moves in reverse if the banksman cannot be seen by the driver.

Chapter 5

Accidents with flammable liquids

The vapours from flammable liquids behave in a predictable way but unless those exposed to them are familiar with their behaviour, serious incidents, frequently involving severe burns to the people concerned, are bound to follow.

Introduction

In every type of workplace these days it is possible to find flammable liquids. Adhesives, solvents, correcting fluids, thinners, cleaning solutions, paints, polishes, lacquers and many other commodities may contain a proportion of flammable liquid. In one sense the term is a misnomer because liquids as such cannot burn. It is the vapour given off by them which ignites.

Whenever any flammable liquid is put into an open vessel exposed to the atmosphere it will vaporise or evaporate. The inherent characteristic of a liquid to evaporate is called its volatility. Some flammable liquids, such as ether, evaporate quickly and are said to be highly volatile. Others, such as paraffin or lubricating oil, are much less volatile. It is a matter of degree. Vaporisation rates are increased by air movement and by a rise in temperature. Hence an oil which is relatively non-hazardous at normal ambient temperatures becomes rapidly more volatile and potentially more hazardous if for any reason it is heated up deliberately or inadvertently. Most of the accidents described below occur because of people's ignorance of one or other of the basic characteristics of the behaviour of flammable liquids.

It will be seen later that flammable liquids need to be properly labelled, kept in suitable containers, stored under the correct conditions and used with proper care, having regard to their particular characteristics. Finally, disposal of waste liquids and the "empty" containers must be an integral part of any safe handling regime.

Why are there inverted commas round the word "empty"? It is very unlikely that any drum which has been used will ever be entirely empty, unless particular procedures have been followed. Empty of liquid a container may be but empty of all vapour is quite unlikely. The degree of risk of an explosion will depend on the proportion of air to flammable vapour present in the vessel. If there is too much air and not enough vapour to bring the mixture into its flammable/explosive range it will be too lean and no fire or explosion will follow the application of a source of ignition. If there is too much vapour and very little air, the mixture will be too rich, for the time being and again, even though a source of ignition is applied, combustion will not be sustained. Without knowing the nature of the mixture and without testing the relative proportions it is not possible to tell accurately what degree of risk exists. This being so, the assumption must be made that there is always a risk as far as flammable liquids are concerned.

Case histories

(a) *Hospital nurse ether spill caught fire*

A theatre nurse at a hospital surgical unit was using ether in an operating theatre when she spilled some on to her clothes. A little while later a static electrical spark generated by her own under-clothing, made from synthetic materials, ignited her ether-impregnated outer garments and she sustained burns. Similar incidents with fatal consequences are known.

(b) *Petrol leak exploded by welder*

An experienced welder, whilst welding a tail pipe on to a lorry exhaust system, was extensively burned about the hands and face when there was a small but fierce explosion in the vehicle pit he was standing in. His colleagues gave him first aid and doused the fire. The lorry being worked on was not the first vehicle at the pit that day. First thing in the morning a car had been drained of petrol over it and some had been spilled. The spillage had been soaked up with sawdust. Enough heavier-than-air petrol vapour had stayed at the bottom of the pit to explode when the welder lit the torch.

(c) *Blowback from diesel "brightener"*

A boiler attendant was told to do something about the central heating system because on a cold morning it was not doing its job. He obtained a quantity of diesel oil in a can and threw it into the boiler combustion chamber. The boiler blew back almost at once and the attendant was burned on his face and hands. The practice was unknown to the management. What became apparent when the injured man was interviewed in hospital was that he had no idea of the consequences which could flow from the bad practice of "brightening" fires, especially those in confined chambers.

(d) *Illicit smoker's gloves burst into flames*

A paint sprayer who wore gloves to protect his skin from the harmful effects of the materials he used, decided to smoke a cigarette. (Mostly, in the paintshop area, the no smoking discipline was well observed. There were, however, inevitable lapses on occasions.) The instant the match was struck, the offender's gloves burst into flames from fingertip to cuff. The man's hands were almost totally covered by second degree burns.

(e) *Clothes soaked by flammable cleaner*

A man who worked at a solvent bath for cleaning metal parts, dispensed with the use of the large impervious apron with which he had been provided. His own clothes became splashed and contaminated. He forsook the workshop for that haven of the surreptitious smoker, the toilets. When he lit the cigarette his soaked clothes burst into flame and he had to be rescued, badly burned, from the locked cubicle by another worker who had heard his cries for help.

(f) *Molten metal ignited paint residues*

A contractor's man cutting up old machine tools for scrap near to the paintshop wall allowed a molten metal particle to fall onto a patch of paint residue below an opening where an extractor fan discharged its vapour-laden spray from one of the paint booths. A small fire started and tracked up into the duct where there was a great deal more flammable residue. Soon a fierce fire raged through the trunking and spread into the spray shop. There the sprinkler system operated and quickly put out the fire. A sprayer was slightly burned when snatching a partially full can of thinners out of the burning paint booth.

(g) *Spot welder sparked vapour from drum*

A spot-welding gun, during a check, was laid down on the top of a large metal drum. There was a spark and instantly following it an explosive ignition of methanol vapour from the bung free drum. After the first flash a second more serious explosion occurred rupturing the drum and shooting its flaming contents over a wide area. A number of small fires started and the man checking the spot welding gun was burned. The methanol drum had been brought into the room for one purpose by one group, used then by another group as a convenient work-top, and lastly as a temporary resting place for the spot welding gun. Lack of control and ignorance of the characteristics of the drum's contents were equally to blame for the incident.

(h) *Explosion during burning off drum ends*

After lying in a factory yard for four years, some empty oil drums were to have their ends burned off and then to go for baling in a press before being sold off as scrap. A man took out the bung from one drum, which was marked "engine oil" and began to apply an oxy-acetylene torch to the drum. He was injured when it exploded without warning.

Analysis

Accepting that under certain commonly encountered conditions flammable liquids give off vapours which can be ignited, and that there is no instant method of recognising without a test instrument when the danger point has been reached, can mean only one thing. Dealing with the hazard has to begin from the assumption that *all* flammable liquids may have their vapours ignited. Having stated this, there is one factor which can help to eliminate some flammable liquids from the need to take precautions sometimes. It revolves around knowing the flash-point of the substance concerned. The flash-point is the lowest temperature at which there is sufficient vaporisation of a substance to produce a vapour that will flash momentarily when a flame is applied. At a slightly higher temperature, known as the fire-point, substances give off vapour fast enough to support a continuous flame after the original ignition flame has been taken away. Linking these factors with the question of volatility, mentioned earlier in the chapter, it can be seen that a very volatile flammable liquid will have a low flash-point. Conversely, liquid which has a low volatility will have a high flash-point. Therefore, from this, it is clear that those flammable liquids which are volatile at ordinary ambient temperatures are potentially far more hazardous than those whose volatility is very low and whose flash-point is a temperature only encountered artificially (ie in a heater or under other conditions where heat is present).

Precautionary measures

(a) *Statutory controls*
   Volatile liquids with flash-points at or below ambient temperatures almost invariably attract statutory controls.

These normally include licensing for storage and stringent controls over conveyance and use. It is not the purpose of this book to concern itself with legislative detail but to look at the principles involved in accident causation. These are, of course, reflected in the systems of statutory control anyway.

(b) *Practical safeguards*

Most of the precautions to ensure the safe use of flammable liquids are simple in themselves and it is not difficult to persuade people to adopt them once they appreciate the reasons behind them. Whenever flammable liquids are used the quantity removed from the main store to the workroom should be kept to a minimum. The reasoning behind this is to keep the potential fire risk as small as possible. In a way it is more a step to mitigate the consequences of an outbreak of fire than to actually prevent it. Nevertheless, when linked with the further precaution of also keeping the day's supply (taken from the store) in a suitable fire-resisting cupboard or bin when not in use, the size of a potential incident in the workplace is effectively minimised.

Similarly, to keep to a minimum the amount of vapour evaporating into a workroom, all containers of flammable liquids should be kept closed when not in use. Suitable non-spill, heavy-based safety containers are available. Needless to say, where amounts other than small quantities of flammable liquids are handled, these should be piped from storage to the place of use and controlled by valves. Levels in bulk containers should be monitored by efficient instrumentation and controls to prevent overfilling and spillage. Finally, well-rehearsed emergency drills should be established to deal with any incidents (ie: leaks and spills) which do occur. So far these comments have not been concerned specifically with the characteristics of flammable liquids, ignorance of which led to the accidents described in the case histories.

Whilst what is covered in the next section still relates to practical safeguards, the points raised are those where the understanding of individuals is paramount in the avoidance of the accidents.

(c) *Training in hazard awareness*

(i)   Flammable liquids give off vapours which, when

mixed with air in certain proportions, are dangerous because in the presence of a source of ignition they can explode or catch fire.

If such ignition occurs in a confined space (a drum, tank, or boiler combustion chamber) the consequences of the ignition will be more violent and the hazards encountered will be increased because the explosion will project missiles violently in all directions.

(ii) It is wise to make the assumption that there will always be a potential source of ignition present which is capable of detonating an explosion or starting a fire. Consider some of the more obvious possibilities:

—Open flames (bunsen burners, gas rings, heaters, matches and lighters used by smokers).

—Hot and/or incandescent surfaces (electric fire elements; internal combustion engines; discarded smoking materials; light bulbs and their filaments; process plant such as ovens).

—Electrical sparks (switchgear; electric motors; short circuits such as with motor car ignition systems; static sparks such as from clothing made from synthetic fibres and from the flowing of certain liquids through pipes).

—Spontaneous combustion (certain materials left to themselves heat up and can eventually burst into flame).

—Friction sparks or heating; lightning; the sun (especially when its rays are magnified through glass); chemical reactions.

(iii) Some vapours from flammable liquids are heavier than air (petrol vapour is 3 – 4 times heavier than air), so consequently they do not rise up quickly, become diluted to a point below their lower flammable/explosive limit and disperse safely into the atmosphere. It is vital that those concerned with liquids whose vapours are heavier than air should know this. They should also know that vapours from escapes and spills can travel long distances and persist for extended periods especially in pits, gullies and drains below floor level and remain in a highly dangerous condition for a considerable time.

(iv) Liquid spills and contamination can be seen and therefore they serve as positive reminders to those concerned to take action. It is vital, however, to understand that vapours can impregnate clothing, gloves, pervious aprons, wiping cloths and any other fabric and that such fabrics will continue to be dangerous for a considerable time when brought near to a source of ignition.

(v) The bad practice of using flammable liquids to enhance or accelerate burning (in furnaces, stoves or on bonfires) should be stamped out.

(vi) No flammable liquid should ever be put into a vessel or container which is not clearly labelled with the name of the substance and with the fact that it is highly flammable (NB the word inflammable is synonymous with flammable but is now seen less and less).

(vii) The practice of smoking needs to be stringently controlled where it can be hazardous. Those areas where it is prohibited (often by law) must be clearly designated. Other areas where it is permitted should be equally well signposted and adequate facilities provided for discarding cigarette ends and matches and knocking out pipe-ash safely. The worst possible position is to have a nominal smoking ban and drive the habit into places where it is hoped it may not be noticed or discovered.

(viii) Especially with regard to smoking, there should be liaison with visiting contractors unused to the rules. They should know where, and if, they are permitted to smoke.

It is also appropriate to remind everyone at this stage that contractors may bring employees on to a site where all the points in this section are relevant. Some managerial procedure should exist to check on the hazard awareness of all visitors.

In conclusion, there are a number of matters which though not directly connected with physical accidents, are relevant in the context of the general health and safety of employees.

Many flammable liquids have a distinctive smell. This should never be relied on as a means either of identifying the existence of the vapour in the atmosphere or of estimating its concentration. The sense of smell tires quickly and is totally unreliable as an indicator of danger. That is not to say, of course, that if something is detected by smell the appropriate investigation should not be made. It should.

The vapours of many liquids are not only flammable *they are also toxic*. It may be comforting to know that if such airborne vapours are controlled to the extent necessary to prevent them being a health hazard they will generally be below their lower explosive/flammable levels.

A word of warning: some flammable liquids which are toxic can be absorbed through the unbroken skin and even those which are not toxic may, by degreasing the skin, precipitate the commonest of all industrial diseases, dermatitis.

Management action plan

(a) Maintain an inventory of all flammable liquids stored, conveyed and used on the premises (including those brought in by contractors when relevant).

(b) Ensure all flammable liquid containers are appropriately labelled, maintained in good condition and kept closed when not is use.

(c) Review all potential sources of ignition and control them by the appropriate means.

(d) Plan work systems so as to keep at a minimum level the amount of flammable liquids present in workplaces for any reason.

(e) Establish and rehearse procedures for dealing with leaks and spillage involving flammable liquids.

(f) Acquaint all staff with the physical characteristics of the particular flammable liquids handled and their significance. Include references to toxic and adverse skin effects.

(g) Outlaw bad practices (eg: smoking, brightening fires).

Chapter 6

Accidents in confined spaces

In confined spaces where people have to go to work, they may encounter sudden or slower and more insidious changes for the worse in the respirable quality of the atmosphere. It is essential to know all the possible origins of such airborne toxic contaminants, their effects and the procedures to counter the risks they bring.

Introduction

It is natural to assume that in the place where we work the air will be safe to breathe. Most of the time it is but sometimes it is not. For a variety of reasons the workplace atmosphere may become contaminated and unfit to breathe. What has been said so far is true of every workplace, but the consequences of adverse changes in the composition of the atmosphere are potentially much more serious when the workplace is a confined space. Accident statistics over many years give ample testimony to this. What is a confined space in the context of this chapter? The answer is anywhere where there is a sufficient degree of enclosure of the work area to hinder or prevent any dangerous fumes, present or arising there, to dissipate quickly of their own volition. It also includes anywhere where, for one reason or another, the level of oxygen falls below that necessary to sustain life. It does not here mean a space where danger arises only from an inrush of material and therefore where there is a danger of burial, scalding, or drowning; or where there are machinery parts which may inadvertently be started up whilst someone is inside the place where they operate. It goes without saying of course that both of the last two places may also be confined spaces where the respiratory hazard exists and the need for rescue may arise.

Mention of the word rescue highlights the extra tragic dimension of this type of classic accident. At its simplest the tragedy unfolds as follows. An unprotected worker enters a confined space to do a job (repair part of the machinery; clean out sludge; paint the interior; repair an instrument; etc) and is missed by colleagues who wonder what has happened. He or she is seen lying unconscious in the confined space into which access is frequently restricted and difficult. A colleague goes in to help and is also overcome. Another colleague goes in and succumbs as well. Eventually a properly equipped rescue team wearing respiratory protective equipment, goes into the confined space and brings out the victims. Frequently they are all beyond help.

Case histories

(a) *Nitrogen purge of storage tank – man overcome*
A contractor's man was seen to start removing lagging from part of some heavily insulated plant. The operator

who saw him, as part of his routine for dealing with entry into danger areas, checked the atmosphere and issued a certificate of clearance for two hours. The plant manufactured liquid and gaseous oxygen and nitrogen from atmospheric air by means of initial compression and subsequent distillation. Very high standards of insulation were necessary at the plant, but to rid the insulation of any oxygen pockets that could have leaked into it during modifications that had been made, it was subject to a continuous nitrogen purge. The operator's job, mentioned earlier, was to see that no-one was exposed to risk from the nitrogen hence the two-hour certificate after the test. The certificate was restricted to the general area where the contractor's man was first seen. It did not extend to the storage tank and it certainly did not extend to the five foot space inside the tank between the upper level of insulation (which had settled over the years) and the top shell of the tank. It has to be assumed that one of the contractor's men entered the space for some reason and that a colleague followed either initially (in which case both were overcome at the same time) or later when attempting an abortive rescue. A third man attempting a rescue on a line was pulled out in time, but he had been overcome within seconds of entry. A rescue team from a nearby works with suitable breathing apparatus eventually recovered the bodies.

(b) *Slurry unblocking job killed two farm workers*

A double fatality also occurred when a farmer was asphyxiated after he went to the rescue of his employee who had collapsed while unblocking an underground slurry reception tank. In a separate, but similar, accident a farm worker was asphyxiated when he entered a slurry channel in a pig farrowing house. Moist green grass and slurry give off gases that drive out oxygen leaving a dangerous unbreathable atmosphere.

(c) *Nitrous fumes in brewery vat from cleaning paste*

A brewery worker used an unauthorised acid solution inside an "underback" (a large copper vessel) to clean it. He used nitric acid for speed rather than the customary paste of pumice and tartaric acid which was used when the routine cleaning with a mild alkali solution was not sufficient to remove difficult patches. Soon after the man returned home from the brewery, his work done in record time, he became very ill. The hospital consulted the brewery and were told what materials were normally used. No mention was made of the nitric acid until the man's wife referred to it as something her husband had told her. Once it became apparent that the man was suffering from the effects of nitrous fumes the correct treatment was given just in time and he recovered.

(d) *Fumes in sewage works chamber overcame cleaner*
A cleaner was overcome by a mixture of carbon dioxide and hydrogen sulphide while doing a routine job at a sewage works in an open chamber below ground level. Two rescuers were overcome but subsequently recovered. The cleaner did not. The job had been done every day for years without mishap. The local brewery had been on strike prior to the incident which might have caused the effluent releases to be abnormal.

(e) *Fitter asphyxiated in tank*
A fitter was overcome by fumes inside a vessel while he was cleaning adherent material from the paddle mixer blades and sides of the vessel itself. Although equipped with a respirator, the cartridge fitted to it had been used before and was no longer suitable for the concentration of fumes encountered inside the vessel. The man became unconscious and was unable to escape with his life.

(f) *Acid release generated toxic gas in pit*
A cleaner working in a storm water settlement pit removing silt, was overcome by hydrogen sulphide gas. On completion of the work he apparently removed a bung from a drain leading from a water treatment plant to the pit. This released 12,500 litres of liquid containing hydrochloric acid into the pit. The acid reacted with sulphides in the silt and hydrogen sulphide was evolved. The cleaner was overcome by the gas, collapsed and subsequently drowned.

(g) *Galvanised tank fumes made welder critically ill*
Part of a factory hot water heating system included a galvanised metal tank, and when the system was renewed the tank had to go. It could not be bodily removed from its site in the boiler room so a welder cut it into pieces from the inside. The tank was 6 feet square and 4 feet deep and the whole dismantling job was done by the one

man. At the end of his eight hour stint the welder felt unwell. He managed to drive home but later in the evening he was seriously ill and needed prompt medical attention, including oxygen administration. Apart from zinc fume fever symptoms, he showed clear evidence of delayed pulmonary oedema (fluid in the lungs). Such an effect, with the delayed onset, is typical of poisoning by nitrous fumes. The combination of zinc fumes from the tank's galvanised coating and nitrous fumes from the welding torch created a toxic cocktail concentrated by the confined space and undiluted by any ventilation.

Analysis

In the open air or unconfined workplace, unless an escape of harmful fumes is both substantial and rapid, most of those at risk take to their heels and run away from it to safety. Where the workplace is confined, this instinctive avenue of escape is not available. Herein lies the nub of the problem. In tackling it, the first question to consider is — what workplaces should be regarded as confined spaces?

There are the obvious ones indicated in the selection of case histories, tanks and pits. To these can be added storage bins and silos, ducts, reaction vessels, large workpieces under construction or being dismantled, drains, and culverts.

There are the less obvious ones such as open-topped vessels, tanks, vats and containers especially where there may be a risk from heavier-than-air vapours which will not easily disperse despite the open tops. Add to these closed and unventilated rooms, ovens, furnaces and driers where because of an absence of good ventilation dangerous accumulations of gases can build up and it is possible to conclude that practically anywhere could under some circumstances be a confined space.

The next most important question concerns the origins of hazardous fumes.

(a) The obvious first place to consider is the plant itself. In other words the process vessel contained the danger all along and it was not adequately dealt with by removal prior to entry.

(b) The second possible source of danger is from leaks or escapes from adjacent parts of the plant and equipment to that being entered, which have not been efficiently isolated from it before entry.

(c) The third possible source is from deposits and/or sludge lying in a tank or vessel which have not been giving off fumes actively until disturbed after entry.

A second group of possibilities now has to be thought about. The sources already listed in (a) – (c) relate to a known fume already present in the plant. Other potentially dangerous fumes are created by the activities of those who go into the confined spaces to do a job. It may be to weld or flame cut; to line a vessel, or repair or replace a part of an existing lining of lead, rubber, plastic or other material such as glass reinforced plastic. It may be to brush or spray paint, or to use a solvent or adhesive. Two matters are relevant here — what is the nature of the fume given off by the paint or the adhesive and can anything taken into the confined space react with anything already there and create danger?

Two final important possibilities remain to be dealt with. The first concerns many of the present fuels used in industry which produce toxic gases during combustion. The second concerns oxygen. There may be too much of it as when using oxy-propane cutting equipment. This enriches the atmosphere and enhances combustibility, including the possibility of causing spontaneous combustion. There may also be too little of it, as when a plant is purged with an inert gas to dispel flammable or toxic vapour prior to work on the plant. This is a predictable oxygen deficiency hazard. Less predictable is the shortage of oxygen brought about for example by depletion through the formation of oxidation products (principally rust) in a steel vessel which has been closed for a period. Also, in many confined places associated with drains and drainage, oxygen may be taken up by constituents in the soil or displaced by the ingress of other gases such as methane or carbon dioxide.

Precautionary measures

(a) *Planned entry*
When any entry into a confined space is contemplated, the possibilities of the atmosphere there being contaminated or depleted of its oxygen content need to be carefully reviewed.

(b) *Permit to work*

When the hazards are known and the work method is decided, it is highly desirable to utilise a permit-to-work system. There is nothing complex about such a regime. It is, at is simplest, the breaking down of the operation into clear stages with specified procedures about what is to be accomplished at each stage. Furthermore, before a new stage is embarked on some competent person signs the permit to the effect that the preceding stage has been satisfactorily completed. By such a system, atmospheric tests prior to entry; appropriate equipment for the job in hand; and suitable emergency and contingency measures, can be detailed and written down, so that all involved can see what is happening.

(c) *Prevention of the need for rescue*

Probably the most important single thing to achieve to avoid this particular type of classic accident is to prevent the first person from entering the potential death-trap unprepared and ill-equipped. Otherwise, human nature being what it is, there will always be the brave and abortive rescue attempts which will claim further victims.

Management action plan

(a) Identify and suitably mark with a distinctive sign all workplaces on the premises which could be regarded as confined spaces.

(b) Identify all possible sources and occasions in such spaces when toxic contaminants or oxygen deficiency would be dangerous.

(c) Train all staff working in confined spaces in the possible hazards they may encounter there.

(d) Train and rehearse all staff in the procedures to be followed (eg: isolation, testing, purging, etc) prior to entry into confined spaces and in the importance of maintaining a breathable air supply by appropriate means (effective local exhaust ventilation, respiratory protective equipment).

(e) Equip and train stand-by staff to go to the assistance of those in confined spaces who may encounter difficulties.

49

Chapter 7

Slipping, tripping and falling accidents

Popular belief has it that slips, trips and falls on the level are invariably trivial incidents akin to banana skin jokes. This is untrue. About a fifth of all reported United Kingdom accidents are in this category. The choice of floor surface; good maintenance of it; a good housekeeping routine; prompt repairs whenever they are required; immediate clearance of spillage and suitable footwear, all contribute to accident prevention in the category.

Introduction

About a fifth of reported accidents in the United Kingdom are in the category described as slipping, tripping and falling. The accidents happen on the level and, contrary to the popular belief that such falls are invariably trivial, many have serious consequences for those who suffer them. Even fatal injuries are not unknown. Industries vary considerably in the incidence rate of such accidents. A United Kingdom study (published in 1985 but relating to 1982 figures) showed an average rate of just over 300 accidents per 100,000 employees. Individual industry sectors varied from the highest in mining and quarrying, where the rate was 2280 per 100,000 employees, to the lowest in insurance and banking, where it was 40 per 100,000 employees.

For every slip, trip or fall there is a reason, or more probably a number of reasons. Unless the trouble is taken to find out what the reasons are, it is not possible to prevent the accidents. Unfortunately there is still too great a tendency to look upon slipping, tripping and falling accidents as amusing rather than as a serious and largely preventable source of injury to workpeople on a scale which remains unappreciated by those who could do something about it.

Case histories

(a) *Boiling water urn pulled over*
A 20-year-old packer went to an urn of boiling water in the tea room for her midday refreshment. She slipped on the wet, plastic-tiled floor and, in trying to stop herself from falling, she instinctively grabbed the urn. Instead of being able to steady herself she pulled the urn over. Its scalding contents caused extensive injuries over most of her body and legs. A drip from the urn's self-closing tap was responsible for making the floor slippery; otherwise the floor was in good condition.

(b) *Wrong cleaner created slippery surface*
A white terrazo floor was misguidedly treated by a cleaner with bleach to keep it white and this brought about a powdering on the floor surface. Pedestrians transferred the talcum-like powder to nearby hardwood-block flooring on the soles of their shoes. This had an effect which was simi-

lar to that of applying French chalk to a dance floor. Many people slipped on it and fell.

(c) *Tripped over displaced gulley cover*

A man carrying a large, empty cardboard box did not see a displaced gulley cover which a maintenance fitter had moved in order to clear sludge and rotting autumn leaves from the gulley. He tripped over the cover and badly twisted his knee.

(d) *Carpet slippers no protection*

A woman canteen helper in a bottling factory suffered from bunions on her feet and found that the only comfortable footwear she had was an old and flimsy pair of worn carpet slippers. As she pushed round a tea trolley she trod on a jagged piece of glass lying on the floor and cut her foot severely. The slippers afforded no protection at all.

(e) *Girl stumbled over pallet displaced by truck*

A poorly stacked pile of empty wooden pallets was placed near to where fork lift trucks turned between two lines of storage racks. One truck caught a pallet and displaced it so that it projected into the gangway. An unsuspecting girl from the warehouse office gashed her ankle badly against it when it caused her to stumble as she was walking by.

(f) *Turn in darkened stair caused missed footing*

A setter coming down a winding wooden staircase after fetching an infrequently used tool from the storage loft, lost his footing at a turn in the stair and ricked his back. He managed to stop himself falling but the tool was damaged when he dropped it. The area was dingy, the walls were painted in a dark green colour and the only light was from a dusty 60 watt bulb.

Analysis

In the United Kingdom study referred to earlier, an accident model is presented which analyses the slipping, tripping and falling phenomenon into its constituent parts. This is done in a way which suggests immediately a number of remedies which may be considered to curtail or reduce the toll of such incidents.

The accident itself is broken down into three main events or sections. These are the initiating event, intermediate event(s) and the injury event itself. The consequences of injury can range from a need for minor first aid to the death of the victim.

Prior to the initiating event there will have been a number of contributory factors relating to the victim, to the victim's movements and to the place where the accident happened.

In the first case the victim may have been poorly trained and supervised in what he or she was doing (eg: carrying a heavy or awkward load improperly). Alternatively, the victim's footwear may have been in need of repair or unsuitable for the prevailing conditions; or the victim could have been elderly, have poor hearing or eyesight; or be recovering from an illness and hence not as alert as usual, and so on. The elderly suffer more from slipping, tripping and falling accidents than the younger age groups; there is a direct correlation between age and the incidence of falls on the level.

In the case of the victim's movement, he or she may have been running, carrying tools or materials, or operating equipment in a way precipitating the initiating event (the slip, trip, stumble or over-balancing; or turning sharply and/or awkwardly round a corner).

Finally, the site of the accident itself. The location can play a significant part in bringing about the event. The possibilities are almost endless. Wet weather, autumn leaves, snow and ice, blocked drains causing accumulations of surface water, algae growth, loose debris, obstructions, slippery surfaces, spillages, steps (worn or otherwise), broken, loose or missing handrails, adverse gradients, poor lighting — all these things can and do cause slips, trips and falls. Virtually all of them are preventable by straightforward, simple remedies.

Precautionary measures

(a) *Floor construction and surfaces*

There are many safe floor surfaces and methods of construction. They are suitable for a wide range of activities so that their actual composition is not a critical factor. It is important however to relate the type and composition of a floor surface to its intended use because the two things may be incompatible.

A surface which will deform and become uneven where heavy objects are placed and moved about on it will soon become an uneven surface where the incidence of trips and stumbles is likely to increase. Floor loading is a matter of prior calculation and discussions with architects, engineers and builders. A floor unable to withstand the loads of normal use is clearly likely to fail sooner rather than later.

A surface composed of materials which are affected by chemicals, oil, or solvents used in work processes, is an unwise choice because the inevitable drips and spills upon it will inflict damage to the surface. In some instances, eg plastic floor tiles, the materials of which the tiles themselves are made may resist the spillage, but the adhesive used to secure them in position may not. The tiles will become loose or completely displaced and the resulting unevenness will constitute a hazard.

Areas near to hot surfaces (boilers, ovens, furnaces) need to be able to withstand the heat without deformation, softening or other types of damage.

Where floors unavoidably become dirty with process refuse, waste, deposits, etc they have to be tough enough to withstand the harshness of the necessary cleaning regime.

The surface of a floor can be rendered less slippery by a variety of methods and treatments. Concrete floors can be physically or chemically roughened to increase slip-resistance and various coatings or overlays can be applied to other types of floor to achieve the same result. Whatever treatment may be resorted to, it should be undertaken by or under the guidance of specialists. Not to do this could prove costly in the long run. Sheet flooring composed of materials such as PVC should be welded at the seams. If the sheets are not welded together, dirt can get underneath at the joins as can the water used in cleaning the surface. Bubbling, cracking and wear are all associated with unwelded seams. Welded seams and close butting to walls and skirtings, avoiding angular joins (which is done by turning up edges as a quarter round) are essential to avoid problems at joins while at the same time making possible a much higher standard of hygiene.

(b) *Floor maintenance and good housekeeping*
The standard at which a suitable floor is kept depends on three things.

First, an efficient method of regular cleaning.

Second, periodic maintenance to remedy incipient defects. It is possible to wait until things go wrong and an incident will serve as a reminder of the need to repair a floor. This is a grossly inefficient way of learning, because not only has the defect to be rectified in any case, but the incident might lead to a suit for damages by the injured accident victim and/or legal proceedings by enforcing authorities for a breach of a legal requirement. Periodic, planned, preventive maintenance is the only sort worthy of consideration. Trouble is forestalled by an organised, regular scrutiny of floors, especially where the wear and tear, and traffic (vehicular and pedestrian) is greatest, eg near doorways and entrances and close to turns in corridors where there are changes in direction by the traffic.

The third thing on which the safe use of floors depends is the existence of good housekeeping. A place for everything and everything in its place. Tidy stacking; regular waste removal; marking floors with lines to indicate "go" and "no go" areas; routines to tackle spills safely and immediately; movable barriers to fence off holes (eg access pits, drains, sumps, etc); adequate warnings and notices where appropriate to guide pedestrian and vehicular traffic, are all essential measures.

(c) *Stairs and changes of level*

Stairs are regarded differently from floors. They are means of access from one level to another and are invariably equipped with handholds or rails on one or both sides. One way of looking at a staircase is that it is a structural feature built in a way to provide a succession of potential tripping points for those mounting them and a series of potential stumbling points for those descending.

Everything that has been said about counteracting slippery floors applies to stairs. In addition there should be a uniform height for the risers and a constant depth of tread for ease and safety of ascent and descent. Any lack of uniformity, especially with half-landings and turns (where the tread plan becomes a tapering wedge shape), can easily precipitate a trip, slip or fall, even to those who use the stairs frequently. For those not familiar with them the likelihood of mishap is higher and the need for a secure handhold is all the more important.

(d) *Footwear*

The provision of good footwear (not necessarily specially designed safety footwear) where harsh or special conditions warrant it, is an important second line of defence in the prevention of slipping, tripping and falling. It should be part of everyone's management policy to insist on the use of appropriate footwear, maintained in good repair. Part of the employees' duty to take reasonable care of their own health and safety must include being properly dressed and shod for the jobs they do. Where special hazardous conditions are encountered such as with chemicals, damp conditions, electricity, molten metal and the handling of heavy objects then it is part of the employer's duty of care to employees to provide appropriate protection for their feet.

Management action plan

(a) Ensure all floor surfaces are appropriately chosen for the work being carried out upon them.

(b) Establish a regular practice of examination of stairways and floors for signs indicating that preventive maintenance is required.

(c) Insist on a good housekeeping policy and require all shop-floor supervisors to give priority to its meticulous implementation in their departments.

(d) Instigate an effective procedure for immediate clearance of spillages and the safe disposal of materials collected.

(e) Introduce and sustain a policy of awareness of slipping, tripping and falling accidents and provide economic inducements to staff to obtain good standard, safety footwear wherever conditions warrant it.

Chapter 8

Accidents occurring during maintenance operations

Every premises undertakes maintenance work on the fabric of its buildings and to the plant and equipment inside. Since maintenance is spasmodic and can often be done in places where work does not normally take place, the hazards are less familiar and accidents more frequent. This applies equally to employees and outside contractors.

Introduction

A United Kingdom study of fatal accidents has revealed that nearly a quarter of them occur during maintenance activities. "Maintenance is an indispensable facet of all sectors of industry," says the study. "Individual operations may take a relatively short time or be intermittent, yet most people will come into contact with maintenance activities at work or elsewhere." In particular, two activities claim many lives: plant and machinery maintenance, and roof work.

The study concluded that over 80% of the accidents could have been eliminated by taking reasonably practicable precautions, and that in nearly 70% of the cases positive management action could have saved lives.

The causes of the accidents most commonly identified were lack of safe systems of work; failure to provide physical safeguards; poor management organisation; inadequate information and training of those concerned. The types of accident were as follows, in descending order of frequency of cause: falls (49%); crushed or entangled in plant or machinery (24.5%); asphyxiation, drowning and gassing (8.5%); electrocution (7%); burns (5.5%); impact (3.5%); struck by falling object (2%).

Discounting the last three categories, accounting for only approximately one in ten of the deaths, there is a clear challenge to employers to tackle the major problems of accidents during maintenance: falls; becoming trapped in machinery; unexpected involvement with the life-threatening hazards of lack of oxygen, or the presence of toxic gases or fumes, water or a lethal electric current.

The temptation to identify human error as the underlying reason behind many fatalities has to be resisted, according to the study. Only when the full chain of events is established by thorough investigation can appropriate steps be taken to prevent a recurrence. It is too easy and quite unacceptable to put the events down to human error and dismiss them as being unpreventable.

It will be appreciated at this juncture that earlier chapters covering the subjects of machinery entanglement (Chapter 2), ladder accidents (Chapter 3), accidents with flammable liquids (Chapter 5) and accidents in confined spaces (Chapter 6), could all apply to maintenance activities as well as to normal production ones. This chapter on maintenance accidents is included to reinforce the need for special attention to be given to maintenance operations because they have assumed such a forbidding position in the accident statistics tables. Why is this so?

A number of reasons are suggested. Maintenance is an irregular, spasmodic activity with which people at work seldom get familiar. Their experience of the snags, pitfalls and shortcomings involved is limited because of this. Maintenance and repair work often takes people into unfamiliar and unusual places to which access was not contemplated when the plant or equipment concerned was first built or installed. Maintenance is frequently carried out by outsiders even less familiar with the layout of what they are working on than the permanent staff.

With "one-off" jobs there is always likely to be a larger proportion of the unknown in the job content and because many maintenance tasks are infrequent and of short duration often there is an overwhelming temptation to make do. Difficult access is attempted with totally inadequate resources and equipment. No one bothers to get suitable equipment because it may be thought not to be worth the bother for such a small job taking such a short time.

Case histories

(a) *Unsecured tower fell with painter*
A tower scaffold toppled over killing a painter. The scaffold was neither tied nor fitted with stabilisers and the top platform was 20 feet above the floor. The tower was not high enough so a 10 foot ladder had been placed on the scaffold platform to enable the painter to reach the job. The painter was standing on the ladder when the accident happened.

(b) *Oiler killed by blades inside tank*
An oiler was killed while inside the chamber of a sand mill in a foundry. It was started up, and ran under power. A captive-key interlock-system on the machine door was defective and not maintained.

(c) *Asphyxiated fitter could not get out of tank*
A fitter was asphyxiated inside a tank while replacing a set of mixing blades. He went through a 14 inch opening with a rope round his waist, had difficulty in breathing and

retreated. He then donned a cartridge respirator and inserted an air line between his cheek and the respirator. The cover for the respirator filter was left on in error. He went in again and found difficulty in breathing and was told by the works manager to take off the respirator. He could not get out of the tank.

(d) *Non-swimmer drowned cleaning pool*
A school porter drowned while cleaning the sides of a swimming pool. He could not swim but had not told the supervisor in case he lost his job.

(e) *Manhole entry killed trainee*
A trainee clearance operative entered a sewer manhole 15 feet deep and was overcome by fumes or lack of oxygen. He was attempting to unblock the sewer using a high pressure water jet. The trainee's employers had no atmospheric testing equipment and apparently were ignorant of the need to test the atmosphere in manholes before entry.

(f) *Linesman electrocuted freeing fishing line*
A foreman linesman was electrocuted while attempting to remove a length of fishing line entangled with an 11,000 volt overhead line conductor. The fishing line was metallic and therefore live.

(g) *Inadequate roof stagings*
The working director of a roofing company fell 35 feet while stripping and re-sheeting the asbestos cement roof of a factory. A single timber staging slipped and the director lost his balance. There was an adequate number of stagings available but they had been left on the ground.

Analysis

Since the range of maintenance operations accidents is so wide, analysis as in the earlier chapters is inappropriate. The significance of this chapter is that it should remind people of the particular vulnerabilities of those who undertake infrequent operations in little known or unknown places (many are outside contractors) and who may be tempted to take short-cuts or cut corners because the job is a one-off of short duration and probably needs to be fitted into a tight timetable.

Precautionary measures

As soon as a maintenance task is identified, there should be hazard assessment. This should pay particular attention to safe access to the areas where fitters and maintenance staff have to go and the establishment of a safe working environment once they arrive there. This means essentially the provision of safe footholds and handholds and should, in their absence, involve the use of safety belts, safety nets or the use of specially designed access equipment. There should be a full appraisal of the hazard potential, for example, from dangerous fumes and/or oxygen deficiency, live electrical conductors, and from failure to adopt foolproof methods of isolation of moving machine parts. This should ensure that unwanted movement of machinery, or unwitting start-up by persons ignorant of those at risk from their action in setting the machine in motion, cannot occur.

Above all, the secret of success lies in the initial preparation of a plan and work method. This should be followed by a full briefing of everyone involved. Someone should be specifically appointed to oversee the operation (especially when outsiders come in for specialist work). A permit to work should be used whenever its formal, systematic sequence can add to the confidence of those in charge that conditions and progress are being checked at every stage, and that a stage is not embarked upon until the preceding one is safely completed and this is endorsed in writing by a responsible person.

Management action plan

(a) Identify ahead of time what maintenance tasks are to be done and allocate a time and a responsible person to be in charge of them.

(b) Undertake a full assessment of the work, taking into account all foreseeable hazards and risks.

(c) Pay particular attention to safe access, isolation of the workplace from outside dangers (eg fumes, electricity, water) and the existence at all times of a breathable atmosphere.

(d) Alert those responsible for dealing with emergencies to where maintenance tasks are being carried out.

(e) Ensure that all personnel undertaking maintenance work

are adequately trained in the work being done, are under the supervision of experienced colleagues and are suitably equipped with any personal protective equipment which may be called for (eg goggles, helmets, safety footwear, gloves, overalls).

(f) Where outside contractors are involved in maintenance work, liaison arrangements should be established to acquaint them with any knowledge necessary for them to do their work safely (eg fragile roofs, live cables, radiation sources). Information should be sought about any activities which they may undertake which could affect the employees or premises themselves (eg welding operations which could pose hazards from the welding arc, fumes, molten droplets and the ignition of combustible materials).

Chapter 9

Accidents in the office

Normally considered fairly safe places of work, offices are nevertheless not free from accidents. The relative infrequency of incidents may tend to keep hazard awareness at too low a level. It is this awareness aspect which management needs to do something about. The chapter covers a wide range of incidents to illustrate many areas which management needs to keep under review and adds a section on visual display units, describing some of the real and imagined problems associated with them.

Accidents in the office

Practically every work activity has an office associated with it somewhere. Although rightly seen as a relatively safe environment in which to work, accidents do occur there. Because of their infrequency there is not usually the same awareness among office workers of the accident potential of their workplaces. This is not really surprising, but it does mean that a deliberate effort has to be made to foster the right degree of awareness. This chapter has been written to give guidance about some of the areas and activities where the risk of accidents exists.

Case histories

(a) *Lift engineer killed by balance weight*
A fatal accident occurred in the shaft of an electrically driven passenger lift serving a multi-storey block of offices. The lift cage had come to a halt between floors, with one woman passenger on board. The maintenance department had been called and an electrician was sent to investigate at once to see what he could do to bring the cage to a floor and release the passenger.

Before the electrician had arrived on the scene, another office employee found that the lift had stopped because one of the landing gates, of the old lattice type, had moved slightly. This had caused an electrical contact to open. Not unnaturally, seeing that one of the lift enclosure gates was partly open, the passer-by closed the gate fully again and the lift returned to normal working. When the electrician did arrive he needed to check that the gate control switch was functioning normally. In order to do this at the first floor level he climbed on to the bannister rail of the stairway. From this position, he was able to lean over the top of the wire mesh screen surrounding the lift well and examine the relevant switch to see if he could determine whether it needed any attention. As he was doing this, another passenger entered the lift cage and started it moving to the signalled floor. Whilst the electrician was leaning into the lift well, the balance weight of the lift descended and struck him, killing him instantly.

(b) *Blocked flue fumes kill cleaner*

Blocks of offices which are, during normal hours, occupied by office workers, are also occupied for a time by others who do cleaning and maintenance work. Their hours of work are quite deliberately arranged so that they do not coincide with the normal working hours of the building's main occupants. One woman cleaner at a block of offices used to come in very early in the morning to do her cleaning before the rest of the staff arrived. On one occasion a clerical worker, arriving rather earlier than the usual time, found that she could not open the back door to the offices, which was the customary route into the building. On going round to the front door, she noticed a strong smell of fumes as soon as she entered the building. When she reached the kitchen at the rear of the offices the fumes were unbearably strong. The body of the cleaner was lying on the floor. She opened the windows immediately and called the police and an ambulance. Neither the police, with artificial respiration, nor the ambulance crew with their resuscitation apparatus were able to revive the cleaner.

The inquest found the cause of death to be carbon monoxide poisoning caused by a blocked coal-fired boiler flue. The boiler was in good order but, because of the blockage, the fumes could not escape up the chimney. Instead they entered the kitchen.

(c) *Corridor direct-access caused collision*

A door in a partition separating a room from a passageway gave direct access into the passageway with no intervening space or barrier. As an office worker came out into the passageway she was bowled over completely by a girl running along it on her way to the canteen for lunch. The partition was fitted with clear glass in its upper half and the woman was knocked into the glass. As a result, she sustained severe cuts to her chin and mouth, necessitating the insertion of several stitches and the removal of glass splinters from her eyebrow.

(d) *Unseen glass partition*

A similar collision incident involved a glass door in a vestibule between the main entrance area of an office building and the company car park. In the centre of the rear wall were two glass doors with large hand plates fitted conspicuously so that everyone knew the doors were there. Large glass panels fitted to either side of the doors were not so obviously highlighted. As two office workers approached the doors, one man opened one of the glass doors but the other collided with the glass panel at the side, apparently unaware that the opening was glazed. His nose was amputated and he received cuts to other parts of his body.

(e) *Draughtsman guillotined hand*

A drawing office draughtsman was trimming a piece of cardboard with a hand operated paper cutting guillotine. He had correctly aligned the cardboard with the base board of the machine and started to bring down the blade. He was distracted and very seriously cut into his thumb and left forefinger which had overlapped the line of the cut.

(f) *Winding handle flail hurt electrician*

An overloaded lift failed to stop at the ground floor and continued down into the well. A maintenance electrician heard the alarm bell and, having found out what had happened, went to the lift motor room at the roof of the building. His intention was to wind up the cage by hand. He had just fitted the winding handle on to the squared end of the worm shaft when someone on one of the floors pressed a lift call button to summon the lift. The lift was set in motion and this caused the winding handle to rotate at high speed, like a flail. It struck his arm and he sustained severe bruising and lacerations.

(g) *Unguarded nip takes in engineer*

A maintenance engineer entered a lift motor room to make one of his routine inspections. He had deliberately kept the lift in normal use because he wanted to try and locate a noise that seemed to be coming from the drive. While the lift was in motion he put his hand on the worm-gear casing to feel for any vibrations that would indicate undue wear. While he was doing this he slipped and overbalanced. He tried to save himself and reached out to grab onto something that would arrest his fall and stop him from being hurt. He inadvertently grabbed hold of the traction sheave and his left hand was trapped between the lift ropes and the sheave. As he was trying to release himself, his free hand was hurt. He then realised that he could just reach the isolating switch which he knew would cut off power to the lift. He operated the switch and the lift motor stopped quickly but not before he had sustained very serious mutilations to his left hand and lesser injuries to his right hand.

(h) *Ammonia splashed in eye*

A draughtsman in a drawing office unscrewed the cap of a drum of ammonia solution in order to fill a copying machine. Without warning, the ammonia solution squirted up into his face and some of the fluid went into his eyes. He received very prompt first aid and by the use of copious amounts of freely running water, he avoided serious injury. The drum from which he obtained the ammonia was opaque so he could not see it had been overfilled.

(i) *Cleaner gassed by chlorine*

A factory consisted of extensive workshops and a large block of offices. In the office section several women cleaners were employed to keep everywhere clean and tidy; this included the toilet accommodation. On every shift, the cleaners gathered their rations of the various cleaning materials they needed. For use in the toilets, the materials included a fairly small measure of a popular proprietary bleach and a small quantity of a specifically designated WC bowl cleaner, in the form of crystals. One of the cleaners placed about 4 fluid ounces of the bleach into 2 gallons of water in her bucket. She then began to clean the urinal stalls. She was called away for some time to do another job and, by the time she returned, she had forgotten that she had used the diluted bleach when cleaning the urinal. She put a sprinkling of the WC bowl cleaner crystals into the urinal and immediately chlorine gas was formed by the mixture of the two chemicals. As she was kneeling down at the time, the fumes enveloped her face and she was badly affected by the gas. She was absent from work for several weeks and had to receive hospital treatment.

(j) *Cleaner received electric shock*

Another office cleaner, doing her normal work, thought that the reflector of an office electric fire was in need of a good dusting. The fire was connected by a 13 amp three-pin plug to a wall socket. The socket had both a switch and a neon indicator and the switch was definitely in the off position. The cleaner assumed what all the signs indicated to her, namely that the switch was safely in the off position and that the fire was electrically dead. Even the neon light was not glowing. As soon as she touched one of the heating elements she received a severe electric shock. After the incident the equipment was examined. The neutral wire had been connected to the switch and the live wire had been connected directly to the neutral socket. This left the elements permanently alive even when the switch was in the off position. It was found during the investigation that the switch had been wired up by the caretaker of the office block, who had no clear understanding of electrical matters.

(k) *Cleaning fluid fumes affected printer*

An offset litho printing machine was used in an office set apart from the main one. The machine was in use nearly all day and the blanket cylinder had to be cleaned frequently with a proprietary blanket wash. The label on the can indicated that the contents included perchloroethylene and that the wash should only be used under conditions of good ventilation.

In the outside wall of the side office, where the litho machine was located, there were four windows. All these windows were kept firmly shut and so the office was always very warm. After a time the woman printer was taken ill as a result of exposure to perchloroethylene and had to receive medical attention.

She suffered from irritation of her respiratory tract, dizziness, nausea, and headache. After the incident the machine was relocated to another wall (also an outside one) and a suitable mechanical exhaust fan was installed so as to prevent the fumes from entering the general atmosphere of the room. Previously no one had read the instructions on the container in which the blanket wash had been supplied. It clearly stated on the label that the cleaner should be used only in conditions of good ventilation.

(l) *Temporary electric fire faulty*

The central heating arrangements in an office broke down and there was a spell of very cold weather. To be sure of having some heat where they worked, the clerical staff persuaded their management to use some temporary portable electric fires which had been kept in a store cupboard. No one noticed that they were in faulty condition. One had no guard and its spiral element was sagging outwards from its supports. The second of the two fires pressed into service during the emergency was without an earth connection to the metal frame because the earth core of the flexible cable had become detached from its terminal in the plug.

The office manager decided that the fires had not been put into the most advantageous positions to give the best heat to the occupants of the office. With the supply switched on, he lifted a fire in each hand and started to walk along with them to what he thought were better positions. The unguarded element in the one fire touched the unearthed metal frame of the other and the manager received a very severe hand-to-hand electric shock which inflicted extensive burning to his hands. One of the effects of the shock he received was to cause him to fall, in the process of which he sustained a dislocated shoulder.

(m) *Boiler explosion*

Many offices still obtain their heating from hot water boilers. Very occasionally one of them is involved in an explosion. One such explosion happened as follows.

The boiler had been designed in the first instance to burn solid fuel but had been converted to oil firing. A gas torch was provided for purposes of ignition. On one occasion when the boiler attendant, following his normal drill, turned on the fuel control valve, there was an explosion as he applied the gas torch to the jets and he was flung backwards. He had been given only the very sketchiest of instructions, although his manager possessed more detailed information. No one ever established the exact cause of the explosion but it was probably attributable to one of two reasons. Possibly, when originally supplied, the boiler had been fitted with a damper which had never been removed. If the damper had been closed at the time of starting up it would have been difficult to establish a flame in the burner. Under such circumstances gas could have built up in the fire-box and eventually have been the source of an explosion. Alternatively, a small leak of gas from the torch or its supply piping could have accumulated in the fire-box and an explosion have ensued when the attendant lit the torch. The full version of the instructions clearly stated that the damper must be fully opened for the starting-up operation. The attendant did not know this.

(n) *Hair caught in rollers*

Small offset litho printing machines appear in many offices and they feature in a number of accidents each year. The dangerous parts of these can be divided into three groups: gear wheels and chain and sprocket drives, in-running nips between various rollers and cylinders and traps between the gaps in cylinders and fixed parts of the machine.

A young office worker, accustomed to working at the printer, noticed that the finished sheets were showing smudges as they emerged from the machine. She did not stop the machine but raised the hinged metal guard covering the inking rollers in order to look closely at the plate cylinder. She had long hair and while she was leaning forward some strands of her hair became caught between the rollers and pulled her head down towards the machine. She managed to reach the stop button and therefore was able to prevent her injuries from being more serious than some lost hair, bruising and shock.

(o) *Trapped in litho cylinder gap*

On another litho printing machine the cylinder gap trap injured a woman operator who wanted to adjust the ejector wheels whose purpose it is to hold the paper down as it is leaving the machine. The feed end of the machine was securely guarded but there were no guards in position at the delivery end. The operator decided to make the adjustments while the machine stayed switched on and running. Her right hand was trapped in the gap in the blanket cylinder and one finger was badly torn and the others severely bruised.

(p) *Pressure release in baler caused injuries*

It is not only the normal power in machinery that is capable of inflicting injury. In the case of a baling machine accident in the basement of one office block it was the sudden and unexpected release of pressure from within the bale of compressed paper that imparted energy to the machine handle. It rotated violently and hit the operator as he was placing a covering paper onto the top of the bale he had just compressed. He was very severely bruised about the ribs and stomach where the handle caught him.

(q) *Mistook shellac for lemonade*

A man who worked in the maintenance shop of a large complex of offices and shops in a town centre precinct put down a plastic cup in which he had some lemonade. The next time he drank from the cup it contained a shellac varnish mixture which had been used to renovate some wooden fittings. Who had spiked his drink? In fact no one had done so. There was an identical plastic cup side by side with the one that contained the lemonade. Without paying too much attention, the man had picked up the wrong cup and taken a drink from it. Immediate first aid treatment prevented him from suffering from any long term effects, but the story could have been very different.

(r) *Tripped over typewriter*

A middle-aged woman who worked as a part time copy-typist found that she had insufficient light to do her job properly at the desk to which she had been sent. There was a free desk near to a window, so she decided to move to it to get the benefit of the extra light. She carried her machine to the free desk and, when she plugged it in to the electricity supply, found that when the lead was plugged in to the wall socket it hung an inch or two from the floor. A clerk from another adjacent office carrying a bundle of files did not see the typewriter lead and she tripped over it. She fell all her length, cracked her knee-cap and suffered severe bruising to her chest.

Working with visual display units

No chapter on the subject of health and safety in the office would be complete without some reference to visual display units, or VDUs as they are popularly called.

Electrical hazards

Apart from the power supply and electronic circuitry, the functional parts of a VDU consist of a keyboard and a screen on which the visual display is shown. The comments made earlier about the hazards arising from electricity apply to VDUs. Only competent electricians or technicians should install and maintain them and there should be no unauthorised interference or removal of any part of the VDU and its associated equipment leading to the exposure of live metalwork.

The point already made earlier about trailing cables is also relevant here. In this connection it is worth commenting that much specially designed, purpose made office furniture for VDUs caters specifically for the accommodation of cables. The use of such furniture is clearly advantageous and advisable.

Radiation

The next potential hazard which caused much concern in the earlier years of VDU use, was that of radiation. Radiation is emitted by these units, but the radiation levels are very much less than those from the natural environment such as the sun and well below the levels considered to be harmful by the United Kingdom's National Radiological Protection Board (NRPB). The NRPB advises that even if women work full time at a VDU during pregnancy they will receive radiation which, in effect, is no higher than the natural background level and does not add significantly to it. The very latest studies have been unable to show a link between miscarriage or birth defects and work at VDUs.

Fatigue

Most types of work undertaken continuously lead to a build up of fatigue. Work at VDUs is no exception to this, so wherever possible frequent, short breaks, preferably with the individuals concerned being able to choose when to take them, should be allowed.

When people become fatigued, their proneness to accidents tends to increase because they become less able to concentrate.

Eye-strain

There has been no evidence during the course of several studies to suggest that VDU work can affect an operator's eyes or make existing eye defects worse. Headaches and eye-strain can be produced by any prolonged spell of work where the same position is maintained and concentration is required over a long period of time. This is as true of VDU work as any other, but in the case of such work the symptoms may be accentuated by an inferior work environment where poor positioning, inadequate or wrongly placed lighting and noisy surroundings all contribute to the deleterious effect. The VDU screen itself can also contribute to the problems in the visual environment if the image is flickering or drifting.

Environment

Apart from the general matters referred to above, it is also important that operator comfort and posture is carefully considered. This entails the use of well designed chairs and desks with adequate workspace and the siting of the VDU screen and keyboard to suit the individual who is going to work with them.

Screen images should be sharp so that individual characters can easily be read and there should be no flicker or movement and certainly no reflections on the screen from local lights or adjacent windows.

Analysis

Earlier chapters (Chapters 2–6) have concentrated on accidents of a particular category, have given a small number of case histories to demonstrate the nature of the category and a few variations on the central theme. In this chapter quite the reverse policy is followed. A larger number of accident case histories has been given to illustrate the very diversity which exists in accident causes and to enhance the general awareness of them among those who work in offices.

Latest figures suggest, however, that although office accidents have many varied causes, two types of accident predominate. Falls and the handling of goods together account for well over half the number of incidents reported to the statutory authorities. Accordingly, these causes need to be dealt with as separate priority issues. The management action plan with which this chapter concludes reflects the predominance of these two major causes of accidents.

By looking at the figures, the following other categories of accident causes can also be identified. Between them they account for approximately a fifth of the total. They are:

(a) stepping on or striking against objects or persons;
(b) being struck by falling objects;
(c) accidents involving machinery, transport, hand tools and electricity;
(d) fires and explosions.

It is unfortunate that approximately another fifth of the total number of reported accidents falls into the miscellaneous category. This prevents us studying their individual causes closely to learn how best to stop them from happening again.

Precautionary measures

Falls

Much of what was written in Chapter 7 is applicable here. Additionally, however, a careful study should be made of all the occasions when staff have to move up from floor level to reach things at any height. Files from high racks, or books from shelves and stationery from the tops of cupboards are all typical examples of where there may be a temptation to use the nearest thing available as a handy stepping place to gain the needed height. The most frequently used makeshift is a chair which we all know was designed to be sat upon and not stood on. Apart from their lack of stability and usually flexible, soft seats which provide a very unsteady foothold, many modern office chairs have casters or a swivel action and are liable to move without warning and cause anyone standing on them to fall off.

A keen look should also be taken at all steps and step ladders to check that they are safe. An even more stringent look should be taken at those high places where things are stored but need not be. Risks from the hazard of falling should be eliminated if possible by removing the necessity to climb above floor level. If it is not possible to do this, make sure that properly designed stepping equipment is used. The modern versions are mobile for ease of transport, but the action of standing on them retracts their casters and they stand firm and do not move about when anyone puts their weight upon them.

A particular cause of office falls is the high number of power leads draped along the floor to serve a wide range of office machinery which trip people up or cause them to stumble. The remedy which is often adopted is to cover the leads by putting them below carpet or carpet tiles. This may offer what appears to be an easy solution to the tripping and falling risk, but at the cost of increasing the risk of fire from damaged and overheated electric leads lying unseen and forgotten below the carpet. As wear and tear goes on, the insulation is liable to become damaged so that eventually it breaks down and electric arcing occurs with a consequent outbreak of fire. Whilst discussing this aspect of the matter it is as well to mention the temptation to over use adaptors. Exactly the same problem of overheating can arise with a similar outcome.

The only proper way to ensure that there are no trailing leads forming tripping or stumbling risks is to have an adequate supply of floor, wall or ceiling mounted socket outlets.

Handling loads at work

There is an infinite variety of handling accidents wherever people are at work. Offices are no exception to this. Since the problem is so widespread and because existing statutory controls have been found to be so ineffectual over the years, there are currently proposals for regulations based upon two fundamental principles.

The first is the principle of carrying out an assessment of all handling operations likely to be performed in anyone's operations, with the obvious proviso that such an assessment should be kept up to date in the light of changes which may be made.

The second is the taking of all necessary steps to prevent reasonably foreseeable injury to employees handling the loads featuring in the assessment. The only exception to this will be in the course of handling in an emergency with the intention of saving human life.

The necessary steps to prevent injury while handling loads cover five distinct areas. These are:
  (a) the task,
  (b) the load,
  (c) the equipment (if any),
  (d) the working environment and

(e) individual characteristics.

The task

   (a) Minimising manual handling

     Here the idea is to consider whether it is possible to eliminate manual handling by the introduction of mechanical handling equipment. Wherever it is possible then this is an obvious step to take.

     It has to be accepted that it is not always possible but, wherever it is, it should be seriously considered. Some form of mechanisation may be feasible, but care should be taken to ensure that the change does not introduce other risks associated with the mechanical equipment introduced to avoid manual lifting. Mechanical handling equipment itself has to be loaded. It also has to be maintained and there may be dangerous parts of machinery to contend with as well.

   (b) Working level and posture

     Loads which are handled away from the body's centre of gravity require greater strength and joints are less efficient when working at their limits of movement. Any jerking, bending or stretching under such circumstances also makes those concerned much more likely to sustain injury.

   (c) Storage

     All goods should be stored at the best height for safe handling. This is between 800mm and 1100mm from floor level.

   (d) Work organisation

     Factors which should be examined in reviewing the organisation of lifting and carrying tasks include posture, rest pauses and job rotation.

The load

   (a) Characteristics of the load

     Loads vary enormously. They vary in their size, shape, centre of gravity, rigidity, ease of holding or gripping and of course in their weight.

     Over the years attempts have been made in certain industries to set acceptable weight limits. Attractive though this idea may be in theory, it is not very satisfactory in practice. The reasons why weight limits are not the answer to the problems of manual handling are that they can only be satisfactorily applied to two-handed lifts close to, and in front of, the body. Also such limits ignore other factors which are very important, such as the number of times a lifting task is repeated and the stature and stamina of the person doing the lifting.

(b) Visibility

No one should ever be required to carry a load without being able to see exactly where he, or she, is going. This is especially important when the route to be followed goes from one level to another, such as up or down stairs.

(c) Dangerous or unusual loads

Whenever a dangerous or unusual load is being moved special care is necessary to ensure that no injury results from its movement.

Equipment

(a) Handling aids

Where there are suitable handling aids they should be used. Where mechanisation is not possible there may nevertheless be some device which can be used to lessen the fatigue and danger which may otherwise accompany the operation. Typical aids are trolleys, slides, chutes and conveyors.

(b) Personal protective equipment

Some loads handled are too hot to touch with the unprotected hand; they have sharp edges; or they give off dust or fumes. In the first two examples, a wide range of suitable gloves exists to give physical protection. If such loads consist of substances hazardous to health then employers, before resorting to the use of personal protective equipment to safeguard their employees, have to establish that it is not reasonably practicable to prevent the exposure altogether. They then have to establish that adequate control is also not reasonably practicable by means other than by the provision of personal protective equipment. Then, and only then, may they legitimately seek to achieve the requisite degree of protection by the provision of sufficient and suitable personal protective equipment. Whilst this issue is most likely to apply to workplaces other than offices, there are office environments where it could apply.

The working environment
Space, layout and working conditions
Wherever loads are handled, the work area should be laid out to minimise manual effort and allow sufficient space for manoeuvre. High temperature and humidity hasten the onset of fatigue. Low temperatures lead to loss of dexterity unless numbness of the hands is prevented by gloves. Factors such as noise and vibration affect concentration and the ability to grip and a poor standard of lighting is always likely to increase vulnerability to mishaps.

Individual characteristics
Whenever handling is undertaken attention has to be paid to any groups who may be more susceptible to any risk from it but because of the wide variety of individual capabilities it is impossible to lay down rigid rules. Age, sex, disability, inexperience, illness and pregnancy are all factors which may need to be considered.

Stepping on, or striking against, objects or persons

Good housekeeping, good maintenance of floors, the clear marking of access routes and a sufficient element of discipline, would prevent practically all of the accidents in this category (case histories (c) and (d) illustrate this very well).

Struck by falling objects

Wherever work at a higher level is carried out, one of the risks to counteract is the possibility of items of equipment, tools, or other objects, including people, falling onto those at a lower level.

The task of reviewing the risk from this hazard is straightforward, but all the overhead work carried out as a routine must be looked at just as closely as the occasional one-off task which by its rarity is probably the greater risk because potential victims are less aware of it.

Machinery

The case histories (a), (e), (f), (g), (n), (o) and (p) illustrate some of the risks in offices arising from machinery. Chapter 2 is also relevant.

The highest standards of provision of physical safeguards should be insisted upon from the machinery suppliers. Further than this it is necessary to instruct operators in the proper use and adjustment of all guards provided. It is also necessary to instruct operators in the correct functioning of the machine and any guards fitted to it, and insist that any defects or malfunctions in either are reported to management at once.

Both the categories of transport and hand tools are of minor significance in offices. They appear because of the retail and wholesale shops premises included in the sector from which the statistics given earlier were taken.

Electricity

The widespread use of electrical power in the provision of lighting, heating, air conditioning, driving lifts and for supplying power to the huge range of office equipment now commonly found in even quite small premises means that the risks from electricity are universally present.

The risks are well known. Electric shock from a potentially lethal voltage is the commonest. The outcome of receiving an electric shock can vary from a short, sharp shock with no permanent ill effects at one end of the scale, to electrocution at the other. What the outcome will be is always uncertain, and will depend upon a number of varying factors, among which are:

(a) the age and physical condition of the victim;
(b) the route of the current through the body;
(c) the duration of the shock and
(d) the proximity of earthed metalwork with which the victim may make contact.

Not only are there the effects of the electric shock itself to consider but there may also be electric burns where contact is made between the body and live metalwork. An indirect result of the shock may be a fall and injuries resulting from this. Electrical accidents can be prevented by a combination of a well-designed and installed system subjected to periodic examination and maintenance by a competent electrician. To this, needs to be added an absolute embargo on unauthorised interference.

Fires and explosions

Fire is a ubiquitous hazard and exists in every premises. Statutory requirements exist to deal with structural means of escape in case of fire and some other fire safety matters such as fire alarms, fire drills and the provision of suitable fire extinguishers.

Apart from this, those managing office premises have a duty to take steps to prevent outbreaks of fire by giving careful attention to the control of the obvious sources of ignition. Electrical installations should be maintained to a high standard by competent electricians. One of the case histories referred to an incident brought about by a caretaker who installed a socket wrongly and dangerously.

Close scrutiny should be maintained to ensure that if staff are allowed to bring along their own kettles or coffee percolators, etc these too are up to standard and not potentially dangerous cast-outs.

There should be a clear policy on smoking and, where it is permitted, there should be adequate receptacles for discarded smoking materials. If smoking is banned in the entire premises, or part of them, the ban should be strictly enforced. Having a ban without enforcement is the worst position to be in.

There should be a regular routine for the collection and safe disposal of waste paper. Combustible materials should not be placed on heaters. Portable heaters should be positioned such that the heat they produce does not impinge on combustible materials, nor should they easily be knocked over. Care should be exercised with the use and storage of cleaners and solvents. Labels should be checked to see if they are either flammable or harmful, or both. Those in both categories should be used under conditions of good ventilation and away from open flames or other sources of possible ignition such as electrical apparatus. The smallest practicable amounts should be kept in the workplace itself and when not in use the cans or containers, with their lids firmly secured, should be kept in a metal cupboard. There should be a set procedure to clean up any spillage promptly.

Explosions in office premises are very uncommon. Those which do occur from time to time are almost always associated with the heating installations, or the gas or oil with which most of them are fuelled.

Management action plan

(a) For action to deal with falls on the level, see the management action plan at the end of Chapter 7.

(b) Eliminate all wires and cables trailing along the floors.

(c) Assess all tasks carried out above floor level and ensure that all equipment used to provide access to them is suitable, stable and provided with adequate handholds and footholds.

(d) Check where all except the lightest of items to be handled, carried or lifted are kept. If their normal place of storage is either out of unaided reach, or they require undue stretching or twisting to obtain them, consider a better and more easily accessible storage location. (See separate "Handling loads at work" checklist.)

(e) Wherever a workplace or access to it gives rise to the risk of things falling from upper to lower levels, provide guardrails and toeboards to prevent this.

(f) Check that all machines (including manually operated ones such as guillotines and baling machines) are fitted with secure and adequate guards which physically prevent all access to any dangerous parts.

(g) Ensure that all electrical equipment is properly installed by competent electricians and checked periodically as a matter of routine. Encourage the immediate reporting of any defects, but strongly discourage all interference with electrical equipment by those who are not fully qualified.

(h) Establish an awareness of the risks from the hazard of fire. Set up a routine for the effective collection and safe disposal of waste paper and other combustible waste. Enforce a clear policy on smoking, and consider a ban during the last hour of work. Check that heaters are well maintained and not covered by, or near to, anything which they may cause to burn.

(i) Arrange for regular servicing of heating installations by specialists.

Handling loads at work checklist

The checklist given below is based upon one which appeared in the consultative document issued by the Health and Safety Commission as part of the guidance to appear with the proposed Handling Loads at Work Regulations.

1. Have you assessed employees' handling tasks and whether they could be hurt by them?
2. Have you arranged to monitor accidents and ill-health to assess the effectiveness of any improved systems of work?
3. Can you mechanise any of your lifting work?
4. Can loads be made smaller, lighter, easier to handle, rough edges smoothed off, or marked to show how or where to hold them?
5. Can you use handling aids such as trolleys, slides, chutes or conveyors? Is personal protective equipment necessary?
6. Can the workplace be redesigned to reduce bending, twisting, stretching, carrying over distances or frequency of handling? Can jobs be rotated to avoid repetition and constant exertion? Are proper rest pauses given?
7. Can you make the workplace safer by widening gangways, removing obstructions, keeping floors clean and providing proper lighting and temperature control?
8. Has allowance been made for the individual characteristics of the workforce?
9. Is instruction and training necessary? If a training programme is introduced is its effectiveness being monitored?
10. Do any jobs require special strength or fitness? If so, has this been evaluated and employees selected accordingly.

In addition to the United Kingdom consultative document on the proposed Handling Loads at Work Regulations, from which the above checklist is taken, there are also European Commission proposals for handling heavy loads. A proposal for a Council directive on the "Minimum health and safety requirements for handling heavy loads where there is a risk of back injury for workers" was submitted by the Commission to the Council in 1988. The proposals are still at an early stage of negotiation. It is unlikely that anything further will happen to the United Kingdom proposals until those emerging from the Council are known.

Chapter 10

Effective accident prevention management

To manage an accident prevention strategy every organisation must have a system of recording incidents so as to learn of the weaknesses and dangers confronting it and to which the incidents recorded give the best possible testimony.

"Near misses" can be as important as accidents which actually cause injuries. Information gathered about accidents and incidents, including near misses, can only become available as a direct result of a thorough investigation into the circumstances of every significant incident which finds out exactly what happened and why.

Unfortunately it is not possible to eliminate every accident at work. It would be unrealistic to believe otherwise. Nevertheless, it is possible to establish a simple strategy to keep accidents to a minimum.

The strategy has to be based not only upon general knowledge of the common causes of accidents but also upon experience of the particular pattern of incidents in the organisation concerned.

The earlier chapters concentrated on some of the classic, common causes and suggested the steps which managements could take to prevent accidents arising from them. To accumulate information about an organisation's own unique accident/incident experience a method of record keeping is required. It is necessary to go beyond the information called for to comply with statutory reporting requirements because, generally speaking, they stop short of non-injury events (with the exception of some potentially very serious incidents classed as dangerous occurrences such as fires, explosions, escapes of toxic materials, etc which are notifiable without being associated with personal injuries).

Every significant incident should be investigated. It does not matter whether it actually caused injury to anyone or not. The important criterion by which to decide whether an incident is significant is whether it *could* have caused anyone to be hurt.

Incidents which could have caused injuries but, fortuitously, did not, are described as "near misses". There is no reason to wait until someone is actually injured before analysing the circumstances which led to the incident. Near misses can be a prolific source of valuable information because there are very many more of them to study. However, it is just as much of a mistake to believe that every near miss contains some profound and basic truth about a particular hazard and how to deal with the risks arising from it as to believe that you can only learn valuable accident prevention lessons from accidents in which someone has been seriously injured.

The essential skill is to be able to tease out the facts about an accident which are crucial to its root cause. When you know the root cause, the remedy is usually obvious and easy to apply.

Investigation

The creation of helpful accident/incident records is dependent upon a thorough investigation being undertaken as soon as possible after the event. Every organisation should have a system and procedure for the prompt and thorough investigation of incidents.

The primary purpose of an investigation is to find out exactly what happened. When this has been established beyond reasonable doubt, the next thing to find out is why it happened. When the reasons have been discovered (there is very seldom just one single reason for an incident, in most cases there are several) it is possible to embark upon preventive measures.

Four areas are suggested for close scrutiny. These are, firstly, the area of plant, equipment, machinery or apparatus concerned. Secondly, the degree of skill, training and experience of all the personnel associated with the incident. Thirdly, the degree and style of supervision exercised by management in the area where the incident took place. Lastly, the existence and quality of the system of work and procedures followed in the activities being undertaken at the time of the incident by all those involved.

When the investigation is complete there must be a formal review of its findings, followed by effective action, followed in turn by some monitoring or auditing process to ensure that the effective preventive action agreed upon has actually been taken and is proving adequate.

This means that awareness of the hazard, training, degree of supervision and review of the systems of work being followed, must all reflect the lessons learned from the incident. If this is not the case then the management of the accident prevention strategy is not a success and drastic action is called for to bring about improvements.

Chapter 11

The people who have accidents

The intention of this "postscript" is simply to turn the reader's mind towards the sort of people who become accident victims. Some of the categories into which they fall present special problems associated with who they are and the particular vulnerabilities they possess. It is no use concentrating unduly on the physical aspects of the accident without regard to the human ones. Both have to be considered.

This chapter looks at four different classes of people and at certain characteristics they display which may play some part in any accident story. Sometimes the characteristic assumes a minor role, but in other cases it plays a critical part in the accident sequence. The reason for including this chapter at all is that it may prompt readers to take an extra measure of care when jobs are being planned or supervised. The chapter may also influence the setting of appropriate standards and monitoring whether things are going as planned. The comments are largely subjective ones, based upon the author's experience of investigation of accidents and talking to victims over more than thirty years inside and outside the Factory Inspectorate. The categories of people are: the young, the old, the handicapped and managers (from the shop-floor supervisor to the managing director).

Young people

The young have relatively little knowledge based on experience. They are full of energy and apt to act without much prior thought; they are possibly contemptuous of authority and the rules they have been taught to heed; they are more prone to fool about without too much regard for the consequences of their behaviour either to themselves or others; and they may resist discarding fashionwear for dull, but serviceable, working clothes. They may also shun the use of protective equipment for macho or fashion reasons.

Patience, thorough training, and very good standards of personal supervision of their work are essential where young people are at work. Statistics starkly underline the vulnerability of young people during the early weeks and months after starting work.

Old people

Older workers have skill and experience. They can recall a wealth of knowledge to tackle most jobs safely but sometimes they overlook that with advancing years their reaction times are slower; their physical strength and stamina are not what they were; and that, with the perfectly normal process of ageing, their hearing and eyesight may have deteriorated undetected.

Management must give thought to the effects of ageing on those who work for them. Demands must be suitably reduced as appropriate as a worker's age indicates waning physical ability. This is not something to be ashamed of, although some may think it is. As an earlier chapter mentioned, slipping, tripping and falling accidents claim more victims from the older age groups.

The handicapped

Both physically and mentally handicapped people can be gainfully employed. In consequence of their employment, the handicapped not only benefit economically but the quality of their lives, compared with that in institutionalised, segregated and isolated environments, is enhanced. As far as work planning is concerned, handicapped employees require closer regard to be paid to matters such as access, the negotiation of stairs and lifts, and special arrangements in emergencies. Liaison with specialist agencies for many classes of handicap (eg blindness, deafness) is recommended, because they have specialist know-how and are happy to share it with those managing workplaces employing people with the handicap concerned.

Managers

Some managers may believe that they are above the adoption of precautions accepted as necessary for others who work for them. They should not behave in this way for two reasons. The first is that hazards are just as real whatever position is held in the company hierarchy and experience has shown that, as a group, managers (many of them very senior) become accident victims. In the United Kingdom study on maintenance fatalities 1980–82 referred to earlier, one in every twenty-five of the victims was a director or partner of the company concerned. The second reason is that unsafe behaviour by senior people does not set a good example for others to follow; on the contrary, it sets an atrociously bad one. Those in charge of any work activity should set the standard which others are expected to achieve. There can be no exceptions to this.

Bibliography

The following is a list of selected references containing further information relevant to the subjects in Chapters 2–9.

British Standard BS4275 1974: Recommendations for the selection, use and maintenance of respiratory protective equipment. BSI

British Standard BS5304 1988: Code of practice for safeguarding of machinery. BSI

Cleaning and gas freeing of tanks containing flammable residues, The: Health and Safety Executive (HSE) Guidance Note GS15. HMSO, 1985

Dangerous maintenance: A study of maintenance accidents in the chemical industry and how to prevent them. HSE, 1987

Deadly maintenance: A study of fatal accidents at work. HSE/HMSO

Deadly maintenance: Plant and machinery: A study of fatal accidents at work. HSE/HMSO, 1985

Deadly maintenance: Roofs: A study of fatal accidents at work. HSE/HMSO, 1985

Entry into confined spaces: HSE Guidance Note GS5. HSMO, 1977

Farmer, D Safe to breathe? Croner Publications Ltd, 1989

Health and safety for young workers: HSE 7. HSE (free from HSE Area Offices)

Industrial use of flammable gas detectors: HSE Guidance Note CS1. HSE/HMSO, 1979

Road transport in factories: HSE Guidance Note GS9. HSE/HMSO, 1978

Safe practice with flammable liquids, FPA Guide to. Fire Protection Association, Aldermary House, Queen Street, London EC4N 1TJ

Safe use of ladders, step ladders and trestles: HSE Guidance Note GS31. HSE/HMSO, 1984

Transport kills: A study of fatal accidents in industry 1978–1980. HSE/HMSO, 1982

Watch your step: Prevention of slipping, tripping and falling accidents at work. HSE/HMSO, 1985

Index